HEALTH CARE IN TRANSITION

MEDICAID MANAGED CARE

EXPENDITURES, SCREENING OF PROVIDERS, AND UTILIZATION PATTERNS

HEALTH CARE IN TRANSITION

Additional books in this series can be found on Nova's website under the Series tab.

Additional e-books in this series can be found on Nova's website under the eBooks tab.

HEALTH CARE IN TRANSITION

MEDICAID MANAGED CARE

EXPENDITURES, SCREENING OF PROVIDERS, AND UTILIZATION PATTERNS

GENEVA BARRETT
EDITOR

New York

Library of Congress Cataloging-in-Publication Data

ISBN: 978-1-63485-817-5

Published by Nova Science Publishers, Inc. † New York

CONTENTS

PREFACE

The importance of managed care in Medicaid—under which states contract with managed care organizations (MCOs) to provide a specific set of services—has increased as states expand eligibility for Medicaid under the Patient Protection and Affordable Care Act (PPACA) and increasingly move populations with complex health needs into managed care. States have flexibility within broad federal parameters to design and implement their Medicaid programs, and therefore play a critical role in overseeing managed care. This book analyzes federal expenditures for Medicaid managed care and the range in selected states' payments made to MCOs; selected states' medical loss ratio (MLR) standards and how they compare with federal standards for other sources of health coverage; and selected states' methods for automatically assigning Medicaid beneficiaries to MCO plans. Furthermore, this book examines states' and plans' experiences using federal databases to screen providers; and how states and plans share data about ineligible providers.

In: Medicaid Managed Care
Editor: Geneva Barrett
ISBN: 978-1-63485-817-5

Chapter 1

MEDICAID MANAGED CARE: TRENDS IN FEDERAL SPENDING AND STATE OVERSIGHT OF COSTS AND ENROLLMENT*

United States Government Accountability Office

WHY GAO DID THIS STUDY

The importance of managed care in Medicaid—under which states contract with MCOs to provide a specific set of services—has increased as states expand eligibility for Medicaid under PPACA and increasingly move populations with complex health needs into managed care. States have flexibility within broad federal parameters to design and implement their Medicaid programs, and therefore play a critical role in overseeing managed care. GAO was asked to examine managed care expenditures and provide information on certain components of state oversight of Medicaid managed care.

In this report, GAO analyzes (1) federal expenditures for Medicaid managed care and the range in selected states' payments made to MCOs; (2) selected states' MLR standards and how they compare with federal standards for other sources of health coverage; and (3) selected states' methods for automatically assigning Medicaid beneficiaries to MCO plans. GAO analyzed

* This is an edited, reformatted and augmented version of a United States Government Accountability Office, Publication No. GAO-16-77, dated December 2015.

federal data on Medicaid expenditures for comprehensive risk-based managed care. GAO selected eight states because they used managed care for some portion of their Medicaid population and were geographically diverse. For these states, GAO reviewed state payment data and documentation, including contracts with MCOs, and interviewed state officials. GAO also reviewed federal laws to describe MLR minimums in Medicare and the private insurance market.

The Department of Health and Human Services had no comments on this report.

What GAO Found

Federal spending for Medicaid managed care increased significantly from fiscal year 2004 through fiscal year 2014 (from $27 billion to $107 billion), and represented 38 percent of total federal Medicaid spending in fiscal year 2014. Consistent with this national trend, managed care as a proportion of total federal Medicaid spending was higher in seven of eight selected states in fiscal year 2014 compared with fiscal year 2004.

Total and average per beneficiary payments by states to managed care organizations (MCOs) varied considerably across the eight selected states in state fiscal year 2014. For example, total payments ranged from $1.3 billion in one state to $18.2 billion in another, and average payments per beneficiary ranged from about $2,800 to about $5,200.

While not required by federal policy to do so, five of the eight selected states required MCOs to annually meet minimum medical loss ratio (MLR) percentages—standards that ensure a certain proportion of payments are for medical care and, in effect, limit the amount that can be used for administrative cost and profit. These state minimums generally ranged from 83 to 85 percent, similar to the 85 percent minimums established in the Patient Protection and Affordable Care Act (PPACA) for other sources of health coverage. All MCOs in the five states had MLRs in state fiscal year 2014 that were above the state-required minimums.

GAO also found that all eight selected states focused on beneficiary factors, such as assigning a beneficiary to the same managed care plan in which a family member is enrolled, when the state selects a plan for the beneficiary in the absence of the beneficiary choosing a plan—referred to as auto assignment. States also considered plan performance, for example, on quality measures and program goals, such as achieving a certain distribution of enrollment across plans. Auto assignments of beneficiaries ranged from 23 to 61 percent of managed care enrollees across the seven selected states that tracked such data.

ABBREVIATIONS

CMS	Centers for Medicare & Medicaid Services
FFS	fee for service
FPL	federal poverty level
HEDIS	Healthcare Effectiveness Data and Information Set
LTSS	long-term services and supports
MA	Medicare Advantage
MCO	managed care organization
MLR	medical loss ratio
NCQA	National Committee on Quality Assurance
PPACA	Patient Protection and Affordable Care Act

* * *

December 17, 2015

The Honorable Ron Wyden
Ranking Member
Committee on Finance
United States Senate

The Honorable Frank Pallone Jr.
Ranking Member
Committee on Energy and Commerce
House of Representatives

The importance of managed care in Medicaid—a federal-state health financing program for low-income and medically needy individuals—has increased over the past decade. Under the managed care delivery model, states typically contract with managed care organizations (MCOs) to provide a specific set of Medicaid-covered services to beneficiaries and pay them a set amount per beneficiary per month—referred to as capitation payments—to provide those services.[1] In Medicaid, as in other types of health coverage, managed care is designed to ensure the provision of appropriate health care services in a cost-effective manner.

As of July 2013, the most recent enrollment data available, about 55 percent of total Medicaid enrollment was in managed care, a percentage that has likely grown since then. Under the Patient Protection and Affordable Care Act (PPACA), states may opt to expand eligibility for Medicaid to individuals at or below 138 percent of the federal poverty level (FPL), with additional federal funding available for this expansion population beginning in January 2014.[2] Many of the people newly eligible under a Medicaid expansion were expected to be enrolled in managed care. As of May 2015, 29 states had exercised the option to expand Medicaid eligibility.[3] In addition, states are increasingly moving new populations of Medicaid beneficiaries into managed care, including individuals with disabilities and those with complex health care needs who require long-term services and supports (LTSS).[4] Increased spending for managed care will accompany this potential growth in managed care enrollment, making effective federal and state oversight of this large and complex component of the Medicaid program even more critical.[5]

States have flexibility within broad federal parameters to design and implement their Medicaid programs and therefore play a critical role in overseeing Medicaid managed care. Under federal Medicaid policy, states can require MCOs to meet standards—similar to those established by PPACA for Medicare and health insurance plans offered in the private market—to govern the proportion of capitated payments that MCOs must spend on medical care and other services, referred to as a medical loss ratio (MLR).[6] States may also establish enrollment procedures for managed care, including procedures for the automatic assignment of beneficiaries to managed care plans when the beneficiary does not choose a plan for themselves, and have some discretion in setting the methods for doing so. In June 2015, the Centers for Medicare & Medicaid Services (CMS)—the agency within the Department of Health and Human Services responsible for overseeing Medicaid—issued a proposed rule to modernize the regulations governing Medicaid managed care, thereby making the first major changes to these regulations since 2002.[7] The proposed rule includes provisions to align standards for Medicaid managed care with those for other sources of coverage, improve accountability for the rates paid to MCOs, ensure beneficiary protections, and promote quality care. For example, it includes provisions related to MLRs and state methods for automatically assigning beneficiaries. While certain new standards may represent a change for some states, other states may have already adopted similar standards in managing their programs.

To better understand the costs and oversight of Medicaid managed care, you asked that we provide information on spending, state MLR requirements, and certain state enrollment policies for Medicaid managed care. In this report, we provide information on

1. federal expenditures for Medicaid managed care and the range in selected states' payments made to MCOs;
2. selected states' MLR standards and how they compare with federal standards for other sources of coverage; and
3. selected states' methods for automatically assigning Medicaid beneficiaries to a managed care plan.

To examine federal expenditures for Medicaid managed care services and the range in selected states' payments to MCOs, we analyzed federal Medicaid expenditure data for federal fiscal years 2004 through 2014 and selected states' payment data for state fiscal year 2014.[8] Specifically, we reviewed data from CMS's Quarterly Medicaid Statement of Expenditures for the Medical Assistance Program, known as the CMS-64 form.[9] We reviewed these data for trends across states and over time, focusing on the federal share of spending for comprehensive, risk-based managed care.[10] In addition, we reviewed state data on state payments to MCOs in state fiscal year 2014 for eight selected states. We selected states that used managed care to deliver care to at least a portion of their Medicaid beneficiaries and were geographically diverse. Our selection also included states that required MCOs to meet MLR standards and states that did not. The selected states were Arizona, California, Florida, Louisiana, Michigan, Pennsylvania, Tennessee, and Washington.[11] (See appendix I for more information on our selected states.) To understand the range in state payments, which comprised both the federal and state shares of Medicaid expenditures, we reviewed relevant documentation for each of the states, including, where available, the most recent set of capitation rates approved by CMS, and CMS summaries of state reported information on characteristics of their managed care programs. To supplement this review, we analyzed CMS data on managed care enrollment as of July 2013, and interviewed Medicaid officials from the eight selected states. To assess the reliability of the federal expenditure data, we reviewed related documentation, including the form used to collect the data and its instructions, and performed manual and electronic tests for outliers or anomalies. We also interviewed knowledgeable officials at CMS about the data set and the form. To assess the reliability of the state payment data, we performed manual and electronic tests of the data to identify any outliers or anomalies, followed up with state officials as necessary, and incorporated any corrections we received. We determined that the federal and state data were sufficiently reliable for the purposes of our analyses.

To provide information on selected states' MLR standards and how they compare with federal standards for other sources of coverage, we reviewed the most recently approved or reviewed state contracts with MCOs for our eight selected states, identifying information on any required MLR minimums and potential sanctions that could be used to enforce any minimums. Where available, we also reviewed state documentation of the methodology for calculating the MLR. To supplement our review, we interviewed Medicaid officials from each of the selected states about their MLR policies and the use of any sanctions. In addition, where available, we analyzed state data on MLRs by MCO, generally for state fiscal year 2014 or calendar year 2014. Finally, we reviewed federal law and regulations, and interviewed CMS officials about MLR standards for managed care plans in Medicare and the private insurance market. To assess the reliability of the state MLR data, we performed manual and electronic tests of the data to identify any outliers or anomalies, followed up with state officials as necessary, and incorporated any corrections we received. We determined that the data were sufficiently reliable for the purposes of our analyses.

To provide information on selected states' methods for automatically assigning Medicaid beneficiaries to a managed care plan, we reviewed documentation of auto assignment methods and relevant portions of the state contracts with MCOs for our eight states, as applicable, to determine the types of factors states considered when assigning beneficiaries.[12] For example, we determined whether the states' methods considered beneficiary factors, such as prior enrollment in a managed care plan, in assigning beneficiaries.[13] We also interviewed state officials about their methods, including any planned changes to those methods. Finally, we collected and reviewed the rate of beneficiaries automatically assigned to plans from the seven states that tracked these rates, generally for fiscal year 2014, and information about how these rates were calculated.

We conducted this performance audit from March 2015 through December 2015 in accordance with generally accepted government auditing standards. Those standards require that we plan and perform the audit to obtain sufficient, appropriate evidence to provide a reasonable basis for our findings and conclusions based on our audit objectives. We believe that the evidence obtained provides a reasonable basis for our findings and conclusions based on our audit objectives.

BACKGROUND

As of December 2014, 39 states were using comprehensive, risk-based managed care in their Medicaid programs. States vary considerably in the extent to which they enroll beneficiaries in managed care versus delivering care through the more traditional fee-for-service (FFS) model.[14] For example, as of July 2013—the most recent enrollment data available—rates of managed care enrollment among states using it ranged from 7 to 100 percent.[15] (See fig. 1.) As is true with Medicaid FFS, states vary in terms of the populations and services included in their managed care programs. For example, some states carve out certain types of services from their managed care contracts, such as behavioral health care services or dental services, and provide those services separately, while other states include those services.[16]

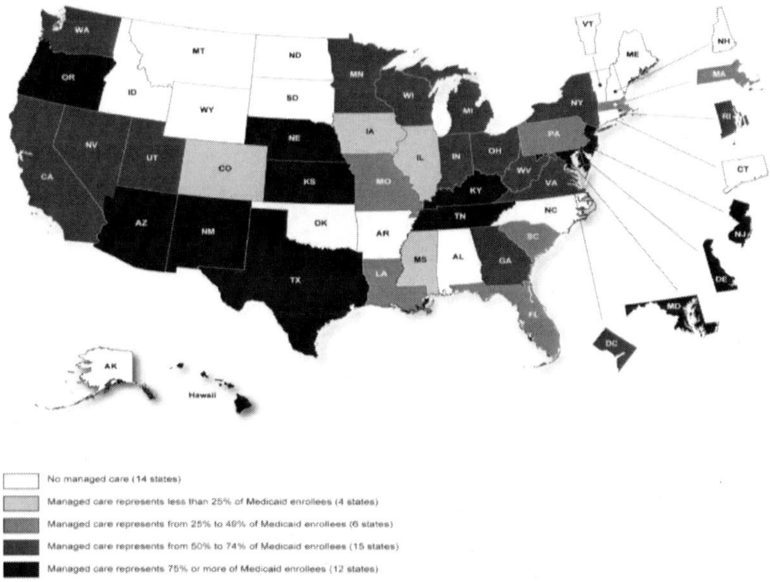

Sources: GAO analysis of Centers for Medicare & Medicaid Services data (data); Map Resources (map). | GAO-16-77.

Figure 1. Comprehensive Risk-Based Managed Care Penetration in Medicaid by State, as of July 1, 2013.

States have the flexibility within federal parameters to determine whether enrollment in managed care will be mandatory (required for beneficiaries) or voluntary (beneficiaries have a choice between managed care and FFS).[17] Further, states may have mandatory enrollment for some populations, but voluntary enrollment for others, and can also transition populations between voluntary and mandatory enrollment over time.

State Methods for Setting MCO Payment Rates

Under contracts between states and MCOs, the state pays the MCO a set amount (or "rate") per member (or beneficiary) per month to provide all covered services and, in turn, the MCO pays providers to deliver the services. In addition to covering medical services for beneficiaries, the payment rates are expected to cover an MCO's administrative expenses and profit. Under such contracts, the MCO is at risk for any costs above the agreed upon rate. Rates must, by law, be actuarially sound, meaning that they must be appropriate for the populations to be covered and for the services furnished.[18] Rates can vary by type of beneficiary to reflect estimated differences in utilization. For example, a state may have different rates for children, adults under age 65, and adults 65 years of age and older. Rates may also differ by geographic region within a state.

Medical Loss Ratio Standards under PPACA and in Medicaid

While not applicable to MCOs operating in Medicaid, PPACA requires that private insurers operating in the large group insurance market, as well as the organizations and sponsors offering coverage through the Medicare Advantage (MA) and Medicare Part D programs, meet or exceed an 85 percent MLR standard.[19] Furthermore, private insurers operating in the individual and small group markets must meet an 80 percent MLR minimum.[20] To comply with these standards, under PPACA, insurers, MA organizations, and Part D sponsors with a relatively small enrollment have some flexibility in accounting for the disproportionate effect of random claims variability (where actual claims experience varies significantly from what is expected) on their ability to meet the MLR standard. While all insurers may experience some random claims variability, the effect of these deviations is greater for insurers with a small customer base.

PPACA mandated a specific MLR formula for private insurers, and CMS rules implementing MLRs in Medicare established a specific formula for MA organizations and Part D sponsors.[21] For example, the MLR for private insurers expresses the percentage of premiums collected (less state and federal taxes, and licensing and regulatory fees) that insurers spend on their beneficiaries' medical claims and quality improvement activities.[22] In general, the greater the share of beneficiaries' premiums spent on medical claims and quality initiatives, the higher the MLR. (See fig. 2.)

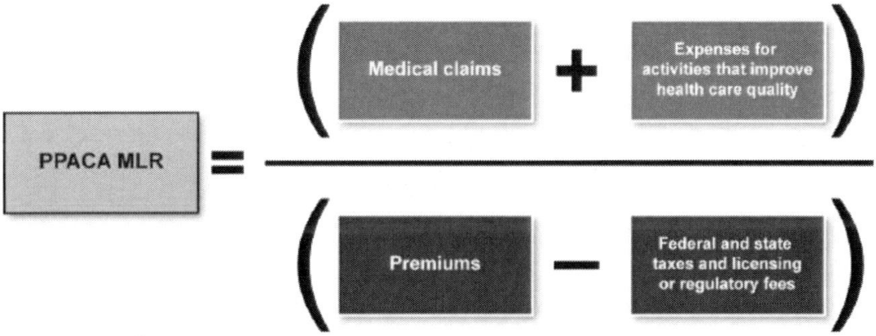

Source: GAO. | GAO-16-77.

Note: This figure represents the formula used by private insurers required to meet the minimum MLR established under the Patient Protection and Affordable Care Act (PPACA). Medicare Advantage organizations and Medicare Part D plan sponsors, which are also subject to an MLR minimum under PPACA, must use a slightly different formula.

Figure 2. PPACA Medical Loss Ratio (MLR) Formula for Private Insurers.

MLR requirements established under PPACA include as expenses for quality improvement activities that are primarily designed to (1) improve health outcomes; (2) prevent hospital readmissions; (3) improve patient safety and reduce medical errors; or (4) implement, promote, and increase wellness and health activities. Insurers are also allowed to include certain other expenses, such as health information technology required to accomplish activities to improve healthcare quality.[23] As such, insurers are able to include expenses for a variety of activities in the numerator of the MLR formula. Examples of such quality improvement activities include case management, care coordination, medication and care compliance initiatives, patient-centered education and counseling, activities to lower the risk of facility-acquired infections, and wellness assessments.

Under these requirements, for each year that a private insurer does not meet the required MLR minimum, it must pay rebates to its policyholders.[24] Likewise, MA organizations and Medicare Part D sponsors must pay CMS a remittance if they do not meet the required MLR minimum in a contract year.[25] MA organizations and Medicare Part D plans are also subject to enrollment sanctions and contract termination after failing to meet the MLR requirement for three and five consecutive years, respectively.

States are not required under federal policy to have contracted MCOs meet a minimum MLR standard. However, states may choose to establish their own MLR standards governing the proportion of capitation payments MCOs may be required to spend to provide medical services to beneficiaries, thus, limiting the amount of payments allowed for MCO profit and administrative expenses.[26] States may also choose to establish their own formula for calculating MLRs for contracted MCOs.

Auto Assignment in Medicaid Managed Care

When automatically assigning a beneficiary to a Medicaid managed care plan offered by an MCO, states may offer beneficiaries a certain amount of time (the length of which is at the discretion of the state) to choose a plan at the time of enrollment. If the beneficiary does not choose the plan within that time frame, the state automatically assigns—or defaults—the beneficiary to a plan. Alternatively, in some cases, states can automatically assign beneficiaries to a plan at the time of enrollment, providing them no initial period during which to choose among plan offerings. The beneficiary is then given a certain number of days after the assignment is made to opt out and choose another plan if they do not want to be enrolled in the one into which they were assigned.

Current Medicaid policy requires states to consider certain factors—with some factors taking priority—in designing auto assignment methods, but also allows states discretion to consider other factors. States using a default enrollment process must give priority to maintaining existing provider-beneficiary relationships and relationships with providers that have traditionally served Medicaid beneficiaries.[27] If that is not possible, states must equitably distribute beneficiaries among participating plans. However, states may also consider other factors, such as a beneficiary's geographic location or the enrollment preferences of their family members.

FEDERAL SPENDING FOR MEDICAID MANAGED CARE WAS OVER $100 BILLION IN 2014, AND SELECTED STATES' PAYMENTS TO MANAGED CARE ORGANIZATIONS VARIED WIDELY

Federal spending for Medicaid managed care nationally increased significantly from federal fiscal years 2004 through 2014, representing over a third of total federal Medicaid spending in 2014. Total payments to MCOs and average per beneficiary payments showed considerable variation across selected states in state fiscal year 2014.

Federal Spending for Medicaid Managed Care Represented 38 Percent of Total Federal Medicaid Spending in 2014

Federal spending for Medicaid managed care increased significantly over the past decade—from $27 billion in fiscal year 2004 to $107 billion in fiscal year 2014—and represented a significantly larger portion of total federal Medicaid spending in 2014 than it did 10 years earlier.[28] Specifically, managed care expenditures grew as a proportion of overall federal Medicaid spending from 13 percent in fiscal year 2004 to 38 percent in fiscal year 2014.[29] (See fig. 3.) A number of factors have likely contributed to growth in federal expenditures, including states increasing the proportion of their population that they enroll in managed care. For example, in state fiscal year 2014, Florida expanded the populations for which managed care was mandatory, which increased enrollment from 1.4 million to just fewer than 3 million beneficiaries, according to state officials. There was also significant growth from fiscal years 2013 through 2014, which suggests that the Medicaid expansion to low-income adults—and the increased availability of federal funds beginning in January 2014—also contributed to growth.[30] CMS's Office of the Actuary reported in 2015 that Medicaid expenditures for and enrollment in managed care has grown in recent years and projected accelerated growth over the next 10 years.[31] The office attributed this acceleration to many states continuing to enroll those newly eligible due to the Medicaid expansion in managed care and the expanded use of managed care to cover the aged and disabled, and LTSS.

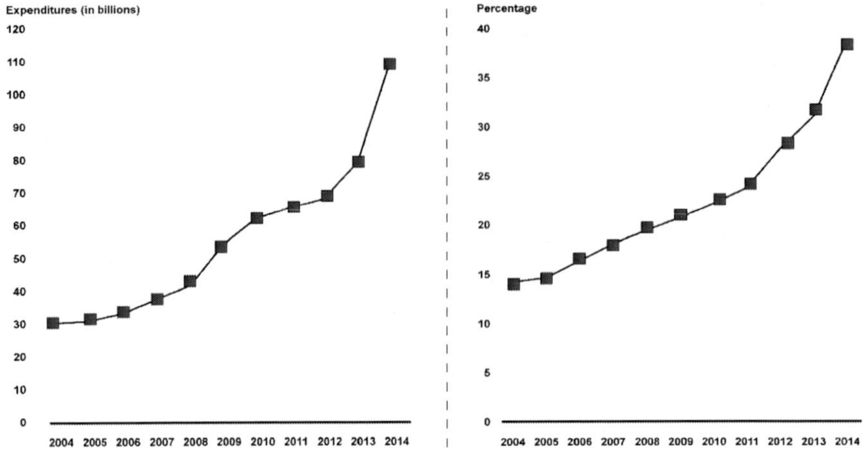

Source: GAO analysis of Centers for Medicare & Medicaid Services data. | GAO-16-77.

Note: For this analysis, expenditures were adjusted for inflation using the gross domestic product price index to 2014 dollars.

Figure 3. Federal Comprehensive Risk-Based Medicaid Managed Care Expenditures, Total and as a Percentage of Overall Federal Medicaid Expenditures, Fiscal Years 2004-2014.

Federal expenditures for managed care varied widely by state—ranging from $5.8 million in North Dakota to $14.3 billion in California—in fiscal year 2014.[32] (See appendix II for expenditures by state.) Also, in fiscal year 2014, federal spending for managed care as a percentage of total federal Medicaid spending varied considerably across the 39 states with managed care. For example, in 11 states, expenditures for managed care represented less than 25 percent of total federal Medicaid expenditures, while in 3 states such expenditures represented 75 percent or more of total federal Medicaid expenditures. (See fig. 4.)

Consistent with the national trend, in seven of our eight selected states, the proportion of total federal Medicaid spending represented by managed care was significantly higher in fiscal year 2014 than in fiscal year 2004, with increases ranging from 17 to 59 percent. For one state—Arizona—the proportion of managed care expenditures as a percentage of total Medicaid expenditures declined from 82 percent in 2004 to 69 percent in 2014. However, state officials attributed the entire decline to a change in how behavioral health expenditures were reported by the state, with the 2004 data including behavioral health expenditures and 2014 not including them. (See fig. 5.)

Sources: GAO analysis of Centers for Medicare & Medicaid Services data (data); Map Resources (map). | GAO-16-77.

Figure 4. Federal Expenditures for Comprehensive Risk-Based Managed Care as a Percentage of Total Federal Medicaid Expenditures, Fiscal Year 2014.

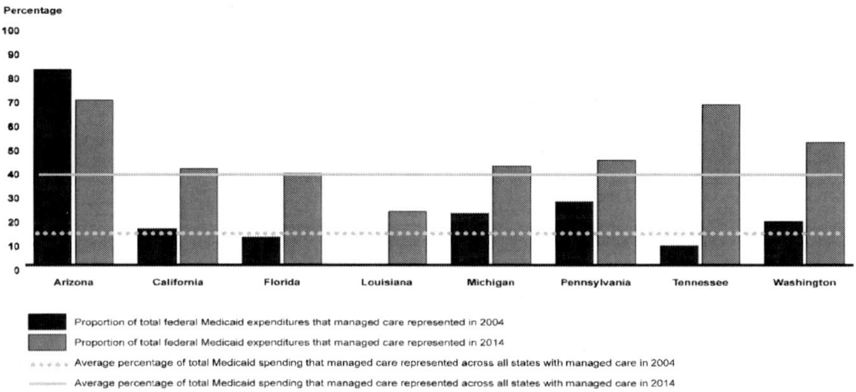

Source: GAO analysis of Centers for Medicare & Medicaid Services data. | GAO-16-77.

Notes: For this analysis, expenditures were adjusted for inflation using the gross domestic product price index to 2014 dollars. Arizona officials told us that the state reported behavioral health service expenditures as part of comprehensive risk-based managed care in 2004, but did not include those expenditures in data reported for 2014.

Figure 5. Federal Expenditures for Comprehensive Risk-Based Medicaid Managed Care as a Percentage of Total Federal Medicaid Expenditures in Eight Selected States, Fiscal Years 2004 and 2014.

Total and Average per Beneficiary Payments Varied Considerably across Selected States, with Differences in Covered Populations and Services Contributing to the Variation

Reflecting variation common in the Medicaid program, generally, state payments to MCOs varied considerably across and within states. In state fiscal year 2014, total capitated payments to MCOs in the eight selected states ranged from $1.3 billion in Louisiana to $18.2 billion in California.[33] Payments to individual MCOs ranged from $17.3 million to $3.1 billion across states and varied widely within some states, with at least one MCO receiving payments above $1 billion in six of the eight states. (See table 1.)

Table 1. Capitation Payments to Medicaid Managed Care Organizations (MCOs) in Selected States, State Fiscal Year 2014

	Capitated payments by state to MCOs			
State	Number of MCOs	Minimum (millions)	Maximum (millions)	Total (billions)
Arizona[a]	9	$107.5	$1,344.1	$4.5
California	22	164.8	3,107.6	18.2
Florida[b]	38	0.01	774.7	4.5
Louisiana	3	401.6	467.8	1.3
Michigan	13	17.3	1,238.1	5.2
Pennsylvania	8	360.9	2,684.5	8.4
Tennessee	3	886.7	2,594.6	5.2
Washington	5	302.8	1,096.0	3.1

Source: GAO analysis of state reported data. | GAO-16-77

Note: In states with multiple comprehensive risk-based managed care programs or models, these data include payments to MCOs in all programs or models.

[a] Arizona's numbers include data for one MCO that participated for only a portion of the state fiscal year.

[b] During state fiscal year 2014, Florida began phasing in mandatory enrollment in managed care statewide. Thus, the data do not reflect a full year of the expanded program, and some MCOs may have only participated in the program for a portion of the year.

The average annual amount of payment per beneficiary also varied significantly across the selected states. Specifically, average capitated payments per beneficiary ranged from $2,784 in California to $5,180 in Pennsylvania for state fiscal year 2014.[34] (See table 2.)

Table 2. Average Per Beneficiary Payments to Medicaid Managed Care Organizations (MCOs) in Selected States, State Fiscal Year 2014

State	Beneficiaries (full-year equivalents)	Total capitated payments to MCOs (billions)	Average payment per beneficiary	Populations enrolled included those qualifying for LTSS[a]	Examples of services excluded from capitation[b]
Arizona	1,206,517	$4.5	$3,766	1	Behavioral health services and related prescription drugs
California	6,552,653	18.2	2,784	1	Inpatient behavioral health and dental
Florida	1,428,520	4.5	3,136		Institutional long term care and inpatient behavioral health
Louisiana	423,071	1.3	3,092		Behavioral health and dental
Michigan	1,371,734	5.2	3,785		Inpatient behavioral health and dental
Pennsylvania	1,620,614	8.4	5,180		Behavioral health
Tennessee	1,174,378	5.2	4,403	1	Pharmacy and pediatric dental
Washington	942,749	3.1	3,259		Behavioral health and dental

Source: GAO analysis of state data and Centers for Medicare & Medicaid Services documentation. | GAO-16-77

[a] State enrollment of beneficiaries who qualify for long-term services and supports (LTSS) into managed care may be limited to certain counties.

[b] Examples of services excluded from capitation payments are not comprehensive; states may exclude additional services. Services may be excluded from the capitation rate for some populations, but not others.

A number of factors may have contributed to the variation in average per beneficiary cost.

- **The populations the state enrolled in managed care:** States varied in the populations they enrolled in managed care. For example, three of our selected states enrolled elderly or disabled beneficiaries qualifying for LTSS in their managed care programs, while the remaining five did not.[35] In Arizona, the average annual payment per beneficiary for the population qualifying for LTSS was $37,700 compared to the average annual payment of $3,000 for all other populations.
- **The services included in the capitation rate:** Some of our selected states carved certain types of services out of their programs and provided them separately.[36] For example, Arizona provided behavioral health care through separate programs for certain populations. In contrast, Tennessee included those services in its program.
- **Geographic differences in costs and utilization of care:** Our review of approved rates indicated that rates for similar populations could differ across states. Because rates reflect a state's assumptions on utilization and cost for a given population and are generally developed using cost data from previous years, the variation across states likely reflects some geographic differences in costs and utilization. For example, payment rates for children under the age of 1 ranged from $416 to $769 per beneficiary per month across four of our selected states that specified a rate for that age group.[37] Similarly, in the four states with a separate rate for maternity care, rates ranged from about $4,960 in areas of one state to over $11,000 in certain areas of another state.[38] Rates also ranged regionally within several states. For example, one state approved rates at the county level and its rates for children under the age of 1 ranged from $416 to $551 per beneficiary per month. In past work, we found that service utilization in managed care varied by state and by population—including whether beneficiaries were enrolled for a full year or part of a year—and that MCO payments to providers for particular services can also vary considerably across states.[39]

OVER HALF OF SELECTED STATES SET MEDICAL LOSS RATIO MINIMUMS SIMILAR TO FEDERAL STANDARDS FOR OTHER COVERAGE TYPES, WITH SOME VARIATION IN CALCULATION METHODS

Five of our eight selected states—Arizona, Florida, Louisiana, Michigan, and Washington— required MCOs to annually meet a minimum MLR percentage. The MLR minimums required in the five states generally ranged from 83 to 85 percent for most populations. The exception to this range was that Washington set a separate MLR minimum for its program covering beneficiaries who are blind or disabled at 88 percent.[40] The required minimums in the five states were similar to the 85 percent federal MLR minimum mandated by PPACA for private, large group insurers, MA organizations, and Part D sponsors.[41] (See table 3.)

The methodologies used to calculate the MLRs differed across the five states with required MLR minimums. These differences in methodology were most pronounced regarding whether the state counted MCO expenses for activities to improve health care quality as expenses that qualify toward meeting the state's required minimum. Three of the five states specifically allowed MCOs to include activities to improve health care quality, as PPACA allows for private insurers, MA organizations, and Part D plan sponsors. The remaining two states either accounted for more limited quality activities—for example, Arizona allowed for the inclusion of case management for its LTSS population—or did not account for them at all. All else being equal, states that allow MCOs to include the costs of quality activities would expect to see higher MLRs. We also found differences in how states defined medical expenditures for inclusion in the MLR calculation. For example, Florida allowed MCOs to include funds provided to graduate medical education institutions to underwrite residency position costs and contributions to the state trust fund for the purpose of supporting Medicaid and indigent care in the numerator as medical expenses.

Three of the remaining eight selected states—California, Pennsylvania, and Tennessee—did not require MCOs to meet MLR minimums, but did monitor MLRs. For example, Tennessee officials explained that the state has routine processes in place to monitor MLR performance. The state requires MCOs to submit annual MLR reports, and according to officials, will follow up with MCOs if it has concerns about reported MLRs. Officials from California told us the state uses MCO MLRs to observe trends for most populations in its managed care programs. The state Medicaid agency does not require MCOs to submit MLR-specific data, but does calculate MLRs for MCOs using their reported financial information.[42] Additionally, in 2014, for the adult expansion population only, California applied an MLR risk corridor of 85 to 95 percent to MCOs. While not an MLR minimum, this risk corridor represented the range of MLRs that the state maintains for the adult expansion population covered by MCOs.[43]

Table 3. State Required Medicaid Medical Loss Ratio (MLR) Minimums in Selected States in Calendar Year 2014 Compared With Federal Minimums for Other Coverage Types

	State MLR minimum	Inclusion of quality activities in the MLR numerator
States with a required MLR minimum		
Florida[a]	85%	Yes
Louisiana	85%	Yes
Washington[b]	85%	Yes
Arizona	85%	Partial[c]
Michigan	83%	No
Coverage types with required federal MLR minimum		
Large group private	85%	Yes
Small group private	80%	Yes
Medicare—Medicare Advantage organizations and Part D plan sponsors	85%	Yes

Source: GAO analysis of state documentation, statements by state officials, and federal law. | GAO-16-77

Note: State requirements are for managed care organizations (MCOs) providing comprehensive risk-based managed care.

[a] Florida's required minimum is applicable to the acute care program. The state's program for the population requiring long-term services and supports is not subject to an MLR minimum requirement.

[b] Washington has two programs—Apple Health Family and Apple Health Blind/Disabled—that are subject to different MLR requirements. The table reflects the required MLR minimum for the Apple Health Family program. The MLR minimum for the Apple Health Blind/Disabled program is 88 percent. The MLR minimum requirement in Washington represents the MLRs that MCOs must have in order to keep its profits and not share them with the state. If an MCO has an MLR between 83 and 85 percent it would have to share profits with Washington. MCOs with MLRs below 83 percent would have to pay the state all of its profits that exceed 5 percent for the year. Washington refers to this as a gain-sharing model.

[c] Arizona includes case management in the calculation of MLRs for MCOs that enroll its long-term services and supports beneficiary population. It does not include case management or any other quality activities in the calculation of MLRs for MCOs that enroll its acute care population.

Table 4. Reported Medical Loss Ratios (MLR) in Selected States, Calendar or State Fiscal Year 2014

State	State MLR minimum requirement	Weighted average of reported MLR	Range of reported MLRs	Inclusion of quality activities in the MLR numerator
States with MLR minimum requirements				
Florida[a]	85%	92%	87%-117%	Yes
Louisiana	85%	92%	91%-93%	Yes
Washington[b]	85%	89%	86%-100%	Yes
Arizona	85%	89%	87%-98%	Partial[c]
Michigan	83%	87%	84%-93%	No
States without MLR minimum requirements				
California	n/a	89%	74%-98%	No
Pennsylvania	n/a	91%	88%-97%	No
Tennessee	n/a	86%	85%-87%	No

Source: GAO analysis of state data and documentation, and statements by state officials. | GAO-16-77

Notes: State requirements and reported MLRs are for managed care organizations (MCOs) providing comprehensive risk-based managed care. Reported MLRs are for state fiscal or calendar year 2014, and may not coincide with the state contract year. As such, they may not reflect the MLRs that were used to assess MCO compliance or to trigger a sanction if appropriate. Reported MLRs were for the following time periods: Louisiana's and Washington's were for calendar year 2014; California's, Florida's, Pennsylvania's, and Tennessee's were for state fiscal year 2014; Arizona's were for contract year 2014; and Michigan's were for the final quarter of state fiscal year 2014. According to Michigan officials, these quarterly MLRs are representative of state fiscal year 2014 MLRs. Weighted averages were developed using enrolled beneficiary months in state fiscal year 2014, with the exception of Florida where the averages were weighted based on expenditures.

[a] Florida's data reflects MLRs for 12 of the 38 MCOs contracting with the state in state fiscal year 2014. During 2014, the state expanded its managed care program, and the state had not calculated MLRs for MCOs added to the program in that year.

[b] Washington has two programs—Apple Health Family and Apple Health Blind/Disabled—that are subject to different MLR requirements. The table reflects the required MLR minimum and the range of reported MLRs for the Apple Health Family program. The MLR minimum for the Apple Health Blind/Disabled program is 88 percent, and the reported MLRs ranged from 98 percent to 108 percent. The MLR minimum requirement in Washington represents the MLRs that MCOs must have in order to keep its profits and not share them with the state. If an MCO has an MLR between 83 and 85 percent it would have to share profits with Washington. MCOs with MLRs below 83 percent would have to pay the state all of its profits that exceed 5 percent for the year. Washington refers to this as a gain-sharing model.

[c] Arizona includes case management in the calculation of MLRs for MCOs that enroll its long-term services and supports beneficiary population. It does not include case management or any other quality activities in the calculation of MLRs for MCOs that enroll its acute care population.

Data provided by the five selected states with required MLR minimums indicated that MLRs were above the required minimums for all MCOs in 2014. Among the three selected states without required minimums, the average reported MLRs fell generally within the same range as the states with required minimums. (See table 4.) Furthermore, officials from the five states with required MLR minimums told us that their participating MCOs generally met the MLR minimums. A high percentage of MCOs meeting the MLR minimums may be expected; for example, we found in previous work that over three quarters of private insurers met or exceeded the PPACA MLR minimum requirement in 2011 and 2012.[44]

If MCOs do not meet the minimum MLR requirements, there are a range of sanctions that our selected states might impose, but officials from the five states with required minimums confirmed that they had employed sanctions related to MLR requirements rarely if at all in the last three contract or fiscal years. Potential sanctions outlined in MCO contracts included requiring MCOs to submit corrective action plans, restricting an MCO's enrollment by freezing automatic assignment, or terminating an MCO from the managed care program. Two of the five states with MLR minimum requirements for Medicaid managed care—Louisiana and Washington—require MCOs to reimburse the state if the MLR minimum requirements are not met. Officials from Louisiana—which requires MCOs to pay a rebate—were not aware of any occasion where the state sought a rebate from an MCO.[45] Washington officials told us that one of its MCOs did not meet MLR minimums for the July 1, 2012, through December 31, 2013, contract, and as a result, was required to pay the state over $4 million.

Information from two states indicated that they also monitor MCOs with MLRs that they consider to be high, because high MLRs could be an indication that rates are not adequate. Specifically, Florida indicated that the state will monitor the financial performance of MCOs with MLRs at or above 95 percent. In addition, although Tennessee does not have a required MLR minimum, officials indicated that they engage MCO representatives about MCO fiscal performance if MLRs are trending above 92 percent, as well as if they are trending below 85 percent. Officials told us the state also used the MLR as a measure to inform their rate setting process, which is done to determine whether the rates paid to MCOs are appropriate and sufficient.[46]

Interviews with state officials indicated that MLR standards are just one of several methods used by states in their effort to ensure that MCOs are using an appropriate amount of payments to provide medical care. Officials from seven of the eight states indicated that they also use the rate setting process, during which states review data on medical and administrative costs for prior years. In Tennessee, officials told us that the state surveys MCOs to obtain specific data regarding their administrative costs.

Officials from several states with MLR minimums questioned their effectiveness and stated that they may not be applicable to all populations and programs. For example, officials from one state with a required MLR minimum explained that if an MCO disproportionately covers an inherently high-expenditure population (such as patients with human immunodeficiency virus), it will be easier for it to meet the MLR minimum than another MCO that has an inherently less expensive patient mix (such as children). Furthermore, officials from two other states with required minimums told us that the potential subjectivity in classifying certain expenses may dilute the usefulness of the MLR. CMS officials told us that MLR minimums are one measure of assessing MCO performance and that MLRs should be interpreted in the larger context. Officials noted that if a state were to set a 90 percent minimum and an MCO reports an MLR of 80 percent, it could be that the rates were set too high and the state overpaid. It could also mean that the rates were set appropriately, but the MCO performed very efficiently.

Selected States' Auto Assignment Methods Primarily Focused on Beneficiary Factors, and Then Considered Plan Performance and Program Goals

The eight selected states varied in their methodologies for automatically assigning beneficiaries to plans offered by MCOs, but all of them first considered beneficiary factors, such as prior participation in a plan offered by a Medicaid MCO.

- Louisiana, for example, assessed four specific beneficiary factors to determine plan auto assignments; namely, whether the beneficiary had (1) family members who participated in a particular health plan; (2) a prior primary care provider who is participating in a Medicaid plan in the state; (3) prior claims history that could be used to identify a most frequently visited primary care provider; and (4) a Medicaid plan in which they were previously enrolled.

- Tennessee's auto assignment method also initially considered beneficiary factors, for example, by re-enrolling beneficiaries who had lost Medicaid eligibility in the plan in which they were previously enrolled.
- Washington's and Michigan's processes prioritized automatically assigning beneficiaries to the same plan as family members.

After considering beneficiary factors, four states—Arizona, California, Michigan, and Washington—also considered a variety of plan performance factors, such as performance on quality measures, in their auto assignment methodologies. Michigan and California assigned points to plans—that is, they gave preference to plans based on performance on multiple measures, such as the provision of well-child visits or comprehensive diabetes care. Michigan officials told us they change the performance measures considered on a quarterly basis to avoid a preference for plans that consistently do well in only a few measures. California also awarded points to account for plan improvement. Beginning in July 2014, Washington began considering plan performance on the completion of beneficiaries' initial health screens. According to state officials, including this measure in its auto assignment methods has been a useful tool in helping the state increase the initial health screening rate among beneficiaries. While not all of our selected states linked auto assignment to performance on quality measures, they all required MCOs to report on quality measures, including nationally recognized or other state-developed measures. Further, six of the eight selected states required MCOs to be accredited by the National Committee on Quality Assurance (NCQA) or other accrediting organization, a process that includes an independent review of the MCO and assessment of performance on quality. (See appendix III for more information on the selected states' methods for overseeing MCO quality.)

Three of these states also considered administrative, cost, or other plan performance factors in their auto assignment methodologies. For example, Michigan assigned points based on administrative measures, such as performance on claims processing. Arizona's methodology factored capitation rates and scores on the plan's contract proposal, with plans with the lowest awarded capitation rate and highest proposal score receiving an advantage in auto assignments. In addition to cost, California's auto assignment method included plan performance on two safety net measures, with plans earning points based on how the plan compares to the other plan scores in their geographic region.

All eight of our selected states considered overall program goals in their auto assignment methods.[47] (See figure 6 for an illustration of a state auto assignment method that considers beneficiary factors, plan performance, and overall program goals.) For example, states made auto assignment decisions based on such goals as ensuring plan capacity to serve additional beneficiaries or managing enrollment distributions across plans in certain geographic markets.

- **Ensuring plan capacity:** Florida, Michigan, and Washington considered plan capacity before auto assigning beneficiaries to plans. For example, beginning in July 2014, Washington plans that received auto assignments must demonstrate that they meet a certain capacity threshold to serve eligible beneficiaries in each of five critical provider types, including primary care and hospitals.
- **Managing distribution across plans:** Pennsylvania divided beneficiaries equally among plans in a certain geographic area, while Louisiana generally did not assign beneficiaries to plans with greater than or equal to 40 percent of total beneficiaries in the state. Arizona's auto assignment methodology had provisions to redistribute auto assignments in certain geographic areas where plans have enrollment greater than or equal to 45 percent of the total beneficiaries.
- **Assisting plans entering the program or a new region:** An Arizona official told us that the state may give preference during auto assignment to new plans entering the market in a particular region. Similarly, California's methodology included specific provisions for new plans, crediting those plans with average performance until the plans could produce performance data.

The rate of beneficiaries automatically assigned to plans, referred to as the auto assignment rate, varied considerably among states. Selected states' assignment rates ranged from 23 to 61 percent, with three states reporting rates of 30 percent or less and three other states reporting rates of 50 percent or more. [48] Rates may vary by population, geographic area, and the method the state used to calculate the rate.

- **Population:** One state, Arizona, tracked auto assignment rates for its LTSS population and reported a rate about 26 percent lower for this population than for all other populations. An Arizona official noted that there is very little auto assignment among beneficiaries using

LTSS because they are typically more engaged in their care and have more outside assistance when initially choosing a plan.

- **Geographic region:** Two states also provided information related to how auto assignments can vary by geographic region. For example, the percentage of total auto assignments for a particular plan in 22 Washington counties ranged from 10 percent to 98 percent. Florida officials also told us that rates vary by region, with Miami having a much lower auto assignment rate than other parts of the state.
- **Calculation method:** Variation in auto assignment rates among states was likely due, in part, to states not having a common method for calculating the rates. For example, Pennsylvania, a state with a lower auto assignment rate, excluded eligible beneficiaries who did not make a plan selection, but were able to be assigned to the same plan as another active family member. In contrast, Louisiana, a state with a higher auto assignment rate, included such assignments in its calculation.

Differences in state enrollment policies, such as the length of time that beneficiaries have to choose a plan before auto assignment, may also contribute to the variation in auto assignment rates. Michigan, for example, reported giving beneficiaries 26 days to select a plan before being auto assigned by the state, while Washington, a state with a higher auto assignment rate, automatically assigned beneficiaries to a managed care plan at the time of enrollment, but gave beneficiaries the option to change plans monthly.[49] Other states may allow beneficiaries to select a plan at the time of enrollment before being auto assigned. For example, according to Louisiana officials, in February 2015, the state began requiring beneficiaries to choose a managed care plan at the time of enrollment, instead of giving beneficiaries 30 days to choose a plan, in an effort to phase out FFS claims processing by the state.[50]

Interviews with state officials indicated that states may adjust auto assignment methods. Specifically, officials from three states told us about future plans to change their auto assignment methods. For example, Arizona reviewed its auto assignment percentages at least annually, and indicated that the state may adjust its method to recognize plan performance on quality and administrative measures, such as those related to claims processing and grievances. Tennessee officials said the state plans to incorporate plan quality and cost performance into its auto assignment process.[51]

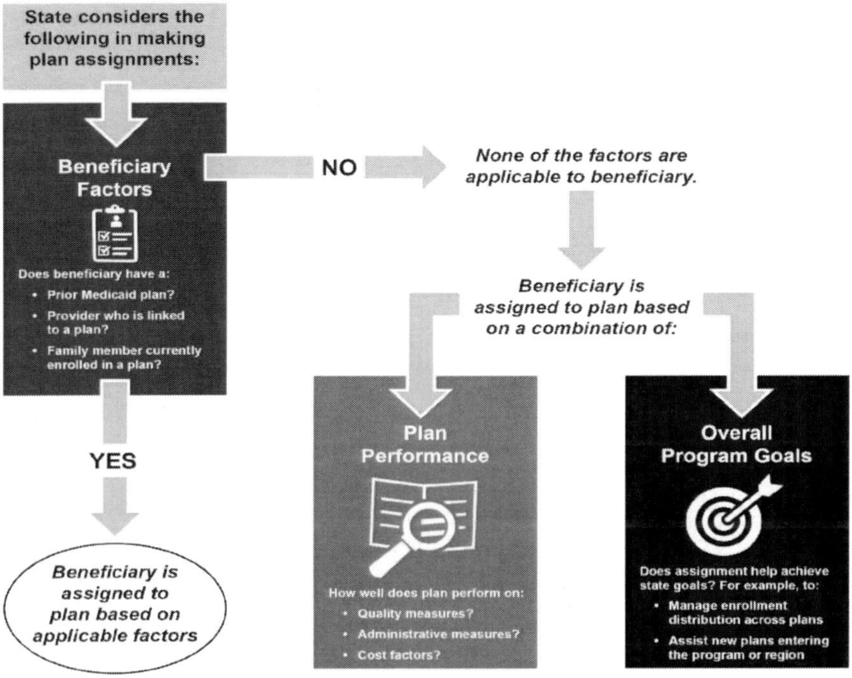

Source: GAO Illustration based on state provided documentation. | GAO-16-77.

Notes: This illustration assumes that the beneficiary has not selected a plan and the state first considers beneficiary factors. If none of the beneficiary factors apply, the methodology then focuses on plan performance and program goals. Not all states may consider all three factors or consider them in this order.

Figure 6. Illustration of a State Medicaid Managed Care Auto Assignment Method that Considers Beneficiary Factors, Plan Performance, and Program Goals.

AGENCY COMMENTS

We provided a draft of this report to the Department of Health and Human Services for comment. The Department had no comments.

Carolyn L. Yocom
Director,
Health Care

APPENDIX I: SELECTED STATES' COMPREHENSIVE RISK-BASED MANAGED CARE PROGRAMS

State	Enrollment as of July, 2013	Contract period	Description of managed care programs
Arizona	1,072,628	October 1, 2014 – September 30, 2015	Arizona Health Care Cost Containment System: Mandatory program for aged, disabled (children and adults), children, low-income adults, those dually eligible for Medicare and Medicaid (dual eligibles), and foster care children. Arizona Long Term Care System: Mandatory program for aged, disabled (children and adults), and dual eligibles, all of whom are in need of a nursing home level of care.
California[a]	5,686,453	January 1, 2014 – December 31, 2016	Two-Plan model: Mandatory and voluntary program in select counties for disabled (children and adults), children, and foster care children. Geographic Managed Care: mandatory and voluntary program in select counties for aged, disabled (children and adults), children, low-income adults, certain dual eligibles, and foster care children. County Organized Health Systems: Mandatory program in select counties for aged, disabled (children and adults), children, low-income adults, certain dual eligibles, foster care children, and American Indians/Alaskan Natives.
Florida	1,516,233	September 1, 2012 – August 31, 2015	Managed Medical Assistance: Mandatory and voluntary statewide program for aged, disabled (children and adults) children, low-income adults, dual eligibles, foster care children, and American Indians/Alaskan Natives.

State	Enrollment as of July, 2013	Contract period	Description of managed care programs
Louisiana	427,713	February 1, 2015 – January 31, 2018	Bayou Health: Mandatory statewide program for disabled (children and adults), children, parents, breast and cervical cancer program population (under 65), low-income adults, foster care children, pregnant women, and aged, blind and disabled adults.
Michigan	1,290,847	October 1, 2013 – September 30, 2014	Comprehensive Health Care Program: Mandatory statewide program for aged, disabled (children and adults), children, low-income adults, and foster care children.
Pennsylvania	1,621,687	July 1, 2013 – June 30, 2014	Health Choices: Mandatory statewide program for aged, disabled (children and adults), children, low-income adults, certain dual eligibles, and foster care children.
Tennessee	3,030,664	January 1, 2014 – December 31, 2016	Tenn Care: Mandatory statewide program for aged, disabled (children and adults), children, low-income adults, certain dual eligibles, and foster care children.
Washington	780,675	January 1, 2014 – December 31, 2014	Apple Health: Mandatory statewide program for aged, disabled (children and adults), children, and low-income adults.

Source: GAO analysis of Centers for Medicare & Medicaid Services (CMS) data and documentation | GAO-16-77

Notes: Descriptions of state managed care programs are based on CMS information as of August 2014 and October 2014. This information is compiled by CMS staff and updated throughout the year, according to CMS. Contract periods are for the state contract with managed care organizations that were most recently approved or reviewed by CMS generally as of March 2015.

[a] California has additional managed care programs, which represent expansions of these programs into additional counties.

APPENDIX II: FEDERAL EXPENDITURES ON MANAGED CARE AS PERCENT OF TOTAL MEDICAID EXPENDITURES, FISCAL YEARS 2004 AND 2014

	2004			2014		
State	Total Medicaid expenditures (millions)	Expenditures for managed care (millions)	Percent of Medicaid spending for managed care	Total Medicaid expenditures (millions)	Expenditures for managed care (millions)	Percent of Medicaid spending for managed care
Alabama	3,237.5	23.1	0.7	3,599.5	0.0	0.0
Alaska	711.9	0.0	0.0	832.1	0.0	0.0
Arizona	4,279.3	3,489.2	81.5	6,565.2	4,513.1	68.7
Arkansas	2,433.7	0.0	0.0	3,615.4	0.0	0.0
California	19,771.8	2,985.0	15.1	35,755.6	14,324.3	40.1
Colorado	1,690.5	228.7	13.5	3,334.8	66.6	2.0
Connecticut	2,477.2	417.8	16.9	3,878.7	0.0	0.0
Delaware	507.4	0.0	0.0	1,003.7	727.0	72.4
District of Columbia	1,016.6	233.6	23.0	1,720.8	605.4	35.2
Florida	9,552.4	1,095.9	11.5	12,151.3	4,632.4	38.1
Georgia	5,336.9	0.0	0.0	6,347.4	2,279.5	35.9
Hawaii	677.9	215.2	31.8	1,125.4	961.2	85.4
Idaho	838.2	0.0	0.0	1,137.3	0.0	0.0
Illinois	6,394.4	127.3	2.0	8,940.5	1,439.7	16.1
Indiana	3,859.8	358.7	9.3	6,144.6	1,274.5	20.7
Iowa	1,810.8	67.0	3.7	2,459.7	69.6	2.8
Kansas	1,371.5	70.6	5.2	1,562.4	1,382.6	88.5
Kentucky	3,613.5	398.4	11.0	5,934.8	3,960.1	66.7
Louisiana	4,427.3	0.0	0.0	4,408.4	981.4	22.3
Maine	1,689.7	0.1	0.0	1,470.7	0.0	0.0
Maryland	2,935.8	840.3	28.6	5,255.2	2,541.4	48.4
Massachusetts	5,579.1	1,006.8	18.1	7,321.5	2,508.5	34.3
Michigan	5,842.9	1,251.7	21.4	9,269.8	3,816.1	41.2
Minnesota	3,557.1	0.0	0.0	5,480.6	2,846.7	51.9
Mississippi	3,178.3	0.0	0.0	3,584.9	602.5	16.8
Missouri	4,721.2	735.1	15.6	5,545.2	675.9	12.2
Montana	620.7	0.0	0.0	729.2	12.3[a]	1.7
Nebraska	1,088.7	48.9	4.5	979.1	261.7	26.7

State	2004 Total Medicaid expenditures (millions)	2004 Expenditures for managed care (millions)	2004 Percent of Medicaid spending for managed care	2014 Total Medicaid expenditures (millions)	2014 Expenditures for managed care (millions)	2014 Percent of Medicaid spending for managed care
Nevada	725.2	107.3	14.8	1,588.7	548.8	34.5
New Hampshire	727.5	0.0	0.0	678.1	122.9	18.1
New Jersey	5,042.0	654.8	13.0	7,099.4	3,534.2	49.8
New Mexico	2,103.0	940.0	44.7	3,139.9	2,463.0	78.4
New York	26,095.4	3,255.7	12.5	27,621.9	12,832.8	46.5
North Carolina	6,326.0	0.0	0.0	7,945.4	0.0	0.0
North Dakota	417.3	1.1	0.3	206.5	5.8	2.8
Ohio	8,655.6	699.9	8.1	13,067.9	6,523.3	49.9
Oklahoma[b]	2,243.8	153.9	6.9	3,037.7	29.5	1.0
Oregon	2,025.0	647.8	32.0	4,952.0	2,918.1	58.9
Pennsylvania	9,785.3	2,569.7	26.3	12,704.5	5,532.0	43.5
Rhode Island	1,172.5	195.6	16.7	1,409.8	771.4	54.7
South Carolina	3,388.2	58.5	1.7	3,770.7	1,565.3	41.5
South Dakota	483.0	0.0	0.0	454.9	0.0	0.0
Tennessee	5,741.5	460.8	8.0	6,064.0	4,054.1	66.9
Texas	12,254.9	1,396.9	11.4	18,790.1	8,068.0	42.9
Utah	1,119.3	148.7	13.3	1,458.8	595.4	40.8
Vermont	627.6	25.7	4.1	901.2	0.0	0.0
Virginia	2,462.8	556.0	22.6	3,843.1	1,314.5	34.2
Washington	3,317.4	603.0	18.2	6,433.9	3,291.8	51.2
West Virginia	1,833.5	132.6	7.2	2,453.9	429.3	17.5
Wisconsin	3,279.2	516.2	15.7	4,447.8	1,064.6	23.9
Wyoming	284.8	0.0	0.0	276.1	0.0	0.0

Source: GAO analysis of Centers for Medicare & Medicaid Services (CMS) data. | GAO-16-77

Notes: Expenditures for 2004 were adjusted using the gross domestic product price index to 2014 dollars. Expenditures include only the federal share of spending and do not include the state share. Expenditures were for comprehensive risk-based managed care.

[a] Montana reported expenditures for managed care in 2014; however, CMS officials told us that the state did not operate a managed care program in that year and therefore reported expenditures were likely an error.

[b] Oklahoma reported expenditures for managed care in both 2004 and 2014; however, CMS officials told us that the state did not operate a managed care program in either year and therefore reported expenditures were likely an error.

APPENDIX III: SELECTED STATES' METHODS FOR OVERSEEING QUALITY IN MEDICAID MANAGED CARE

Our eight selected states (Arizona, California, Florida, Louisiana, Michigan, Pennsylvania, Tennessee, and Washington) varied in the methods used to oversee the quality of care provided by contracted managed care organizations (MCOs). See the table below and the discussion that follows for information on the types of quality measures, sanctions, incentives, and accreditation requirements states used and how those methods fit into each state's broader quality framework.

Table 5. Methods for Overseeing Quality of Care Provided by Medicaid Managed Care Organizations (MCOs) in Selected States

				Sanction types for performance on certain quality standards			
State	Required reporting of HEDIS measures[a]	Required reporting on other measures	Sanctions tied to certain performance measures	Corrective Action Plans	Financial[b]	Incentives for performance on certain measures[c]	Accreditation required?[d]
Arizona	Some	Y	Y	√	√	Y	No
California	All	Y	Y	√	√	N	No
Florida	Some	Y	Y	√	√	Y	NCQA or Other
Louisiana	Some	Y	Y	√	√	Y	NCQA
Michigan	All	Y	Y	√	√	Y	NCQA or Other
Pennsylvania	All	Y	Y	√	√	Y	NCQA or Other
Tennessee	All	Y	Y	√	√	Y	NCQA
Washington	Some	Y	N	N/A	N/A	N	NCQA

Legend: HEDIS = Healthcare Effectiveness Data and Information Set; Y = yes; N = no; NCQA = National Committee on Quality Assurance; and N/A = not applicable.

Source: GAO analysis of state contracts with MCOs, state quality documentation, and interviews with state officials. | GAO-16-77.

Notes: The information presented reflects requirements outlined in the state contract with MCOs that was most recently approved or reviewed by CMS, generally, as of March 2015. Five states' contracts—Arizona, California, Florida, Louisiana, and Tennessee—were effective as of August 2015.

Pennsylvania's contract ended at the end of June 2014 and Washington's at the end of December 2014. Michigan's contract ended at the end of September 2014.

[a] For the states that required reporting on all HEDIS measures, we are referring to the measures that are relevant to Medicaid. These states may not require reporting on the subset of those requirements focused on dental care.

[b] Financial sanctions may be monetary penalties for failure to meet minimum performance targets or payment reductions for performance below the median.

[c] Incentives could include bonuses or an increase in the number of beneficiaries who are automatically assigned to a plan offered by the MCO.

[d] State required accreditation by NCQA or other accrediting bodies.

Quality Performance Measures

All eight selected states used a combination of Healthcare Effectiveness Data and Information Set (HEDIS) and non-HEDIS measures to assess quality performance of their participating MCOs. HEDIS is a tool used by health plans to measure performance on various dimensions of care and service, including effectiveness of care, access and availability of care, experience of care, utilization and risk adjusted utilization, and relative resource use. In the 2015 HEDIS, 68 of the 83 measures are applicable to Medicaid.

- With regard to HEDIS measures, all selected states required their participating MCOs to report at least some HEDIS measures that are applicable to Medicaid. Four of the states required MCOs to report all of the Medicaid-applicable HEDIS measures.
- All selected states either required MCOs to report on specific non-HEDIS measures, or their contracts allowed states to develop non-HEDIS measures that MCOs may have to report. The non-HEDIS measures states required varied. For example, Arizona listed two non-HEDIS measures related to flu shots for adults above the age of 50, while Florida listed 10 non-HEDIS measures, including but not limited to, the provision of annual lipid profiles, the frequency of human immunodeficiency virus disease monitoring lab tests, and transportation timeliness.
- Non-HEDIS measures may capture similar issues as the HEDIS measures, but in a slightly different manner. For example, there is an adult flu shot HEDIS measure applicable to Medicaid that captures the provision of flu shots for those aged 18 to 64. However, there is no adult flu shot measure applicable to Medicaid that is for ages 65

and older, and no way within the existing HEDIS measure to distinguish older adults. As such, to capture older adults, Arizona uses two nonHEDIS measures in their Medicaid managed care program: flu shots for adults aged 50-64, and flu shots for adults aged 65 and older. Other types of non-HEDIS measures that states are requiring MCOs to report include: Children's Health Insurance Program Reauthorization Act child and adult core set measures; over- and under-utilization monitoring measures; Agency for Healthcare Research and Quality prevention quality indicators; and other state-defined measures.

Sanctions for Not Meeting Required Targets on Quality Measures

All but one of our eight selected states set specific standards for performance on one or more quality measures that, if not met, could result in sanctions for MCOs. Sanctions could include requiring MCOs to take corrective actions, financial penalties, or both.

- Six states—Arizona, California, Florida, Michigan, Pennsylvania, and Tennessee—specified in their contracts that there are minimum requirements for outcomes on performance measures that each MCO was required to meet. These states specified that MCOs that do not meet the requirements may be subject to corrective action plans, financial sanctions, or other types of sanctions.
- The final state that set standards for performance on quality measures, Louisiana, required MCOs to demonstrate improvement on performance measures and linked sanctions to failure to meet such improvement.
- The remaining state, Washington, did not include any sanctions that were specifically imposed for failing to meet required performance measure outcomes, though the state could impose sanctions for failure to meet contract terms more generally.

With regard to imposing sanctions, generally, states describe a measured, hierarchical approach, starting first with corrective action plans and imposing more severe sanctions if the MCO does not come into compliance with the corrective action plan. Financial penalties may be imposed along with corrective action plans or as a more severe sanction after the corrective action plan. Financial penalties may be structured such that failure to meet a certain threshold percentage on a performance measure will require that the MCO pay a certain amount for each percent difference between the standard and the percentage it reported. For example, Tennessee set a 5 percent threshold for unanswered calls for its MCOs' nurse triage and advice lines. The state will charge MCOs $25,000 for each full percentage point above 5 percent per month. Some states linked failure to meet certain standards on performance measures to intermediate sanctions as outlined in federal regulations. These sanctions allow for appointing temporary management of the MCO; freezing new enrollments, including auto enrollment; allowing beneficiaries to terminate enrollment; and suspending payment for beneficiaries enrolled after the effective date of the sanction.[1]

Incentives for Performance on Quality Measures

While there was no consistent method of measuring quality across states, most of the selected states used financial incentives as rewards for MCOs meeting performance standards on certain quality measures. Specifically, six of the eight states established incentives for MCOs performing above a certain benchmark or for improving in performance on selected measures, as shown in the following examples.

- Pennsylvania allocated incentive dollars to each of nine performance measures, and MCOs earn incentives by meeting benchmark performance and improvement targets. In addition, if the MCO performs above the 50th percentile benchmark on diabetes bundle measures the state will award a diabetes bundle performance payout.
- Tennessee focused its incentives on performance improvement by offering a bonus payment to MCOs for each HEDIS measure for which it demonstrated significant improvement.
- Two of the six states that offered incentives—Arizona and Florida—specified that the incentives may be competitive.
    - Arizona assesses MCOs relative to minimum performance standards. A bonus is awarded to one or more MCOs for their performance on certain quality measures.
    - Florida's managed care contract indicated that the state may decide to offer incentives to all high performing MCOs or to

make the high performing MCOs compete for them. The state may also decide not to offer incentives to its MCOs each year.

States offering incentives often financed them using capitation payment withholds where the state retains a relatively small percentage of the monthly or annual capitation payments (for example, 1 or 2 percent), and uses it later to reward MCOs that performed well on certain performance measures.[2]

Accreditation Requirements

Six of the eight selected states required participating MCOs to be accredited by a nationally recognized organization that provides an independent assessment of the quality of care provided by the MCO. MCOs that are accredited by these organizations meet quality standards related to various aspects such as consumer protection, case management, and quality improvement activities.

- The National Committee on Quality Assurance (NCQA) was the most commonly used accrediting organization in the selected states. All six states either named NCQA as a preferred accreditation body or only allowed NCQA accreditation. States also may have allowed MCOs to be accredited through another accrediting organization, such as URAC or the Accreditation Association for Ambulatory Health Care.
- In discussions with some states, one reason cited for requiring accreditation was that it facilitated the comparison of MCOs because of consistency of data requirements.
- The two states that did not require accreditation explained that they were concerned about the financial burden on the MCOs associated with the accreditation process.[3]

Other Quality Oversight Activities

All of the selected states had a written quality strategy for Medicaid managed care that they submitted to the Centers for Medicare & Medicaid Services (CMS) per a federal requirement to do so.[4] The state quality strategy must include a discussion of performance measures, performance improvement projects, and state quality oversight plans.

States are required to submit a revised strategy to CMS whenever significant changes are made.

CMS reviews states' quality strategy documents as submitted and does not require them to be updated within a specified timeframe. CMS is proposing to change this; its proposed rule would require states to update their quality strategy documents at least once every 3 years.[5] According to a CMS quality strategy tracking document, some states submit their quality strategy document to CMS annually, while others have not submitted them to CMS for 3 or more years.

- Among our eight selected states, five had submitted updated versions of their quality strategy to CMS between 2012 and 2014, with three of these five states submitting to CMS annually.
- The remaining three selected states had not submitted an updated version of their quality strategies to CMS in the last 4 to 8 years, according to CMS's tracking document.[6]

Nationally, the tracking document indicates that 8 of the 39 states with comprehensive, risk-based managed care have not submitted updated quality strategy documents to CMS in the last 3 years.

As required by federal law, all of our selected states completed an external quality review report in 2014.[7] In an external quality review, an independent organization specializing in external quality reviews evaluates the quality, timeliness, and access to health care services provided by MCOs to their Medicaid beneficiaries. External quality review reports include discussions of MCO's strengths, areas for improvement, and recommendations, as shown in the examples below.

- An external quality review report for one of our selected states indicated that the strengths of the MCOs participating in the state's managed care program were that they demonstrated high levels of compliance with contractual requirements and that they improved in their performance on quality measures from previous years. As an opportunity for improvement, this report also mentioned that MCOs could work to improve performance on certain HEDIS measures for which they were performing below the 50th percentile.
- Another state's external quality review report recommended MCOs identify barriers that affect access to care for children's services after the performance measures assessment showed poor performance in

well-child and dental visits. The report recommended increased transportation coordination and expanded office hours, as well as educational efforts to increase beneficiary awareness and understanding of available services.

End Notes

[1] States may have different types of managed care arrangements in Medicaid. In this report, where we refer to Medicaid managed care, we are referring to comprehensive, risk-based managed care, the most common type of managed care arrangement.

[2] Pub. L. No. 111-148, §§ 2001, 10201(c), 124 Stat. 119, 271, 918 (2010), as amended by the Health Care and Education Reconciliation Act (HCERA), Pub. L. No. 111-152, § 1201, 124 Stat. 1029, 1051 (2010). For purposes of this report, references to PPACA include the amendments made by HCERA. Under PPACA, states may expand Medicaid eligibility under their state Medicaid plans to nonpregnant, nonelderly adults who are not eligible for Medicare and whose income does not exceed 133 percent of the FPL. PPACA also provides for a 5 percent disregard when calculating income for determining Medicaid eligibility, which effectively increases this income level to 138 percent of the FPL. The FPL for a family of four in the 48 contiguous states and the District of Columbia in 2015 was $24,250; 138 percent of this amount would be $33,465.

[3] For the purposes of this report, we consider the District of Columbia a state.

[4] LTSS include many types of health and health-related services, including both institutionally based services, such as nursing home care, and home and community based services, such as home health and adult day care. LTSS are for individuals of all ages who have limited ability to care for themselves because of physical, cognitive, or mental disabilities or conditions.

[5] The Medicaid program is on GAO's high risk list, in part because of concerns about managed care payment oversight and the need for better data. See GAO, *HIGH RISK SERIES: An Update*, GAO-15-290 (Washington, D.C.: Feb. 11, 2015). For additional issues related to Medicaid managed care oversight, see GAO, *Medicaid: Key Issues Facing the Program,* GAO-15-677 (Washington, D.C.: July 30, 2015).

[6] Medicare is the federal health insurance program that covers seniors aged 65 and older, and certain disabled persons and persons with end-stage renal disease. Medicare Parts A and B are known as Medicare fee-for-service. Medicare beneficiaries have the option of obtaining coverage for Medicare services from private health plans that participate in Medicare Advantage—Medicare's managed care program—also known as Part C. Medicare beneficiaries may purchase coverage for outpatient prescription drugs under Part D.

[7] 80 Fed. Reg. 31098 (June 1, 2015).

[8] In this report, unless otherwise noted, fiscal year refers to the federal fiscal year.

[9] State Medicaid agencies submit expenditure information to CMS on a quarterly basis by means of the CMS-64 form within the Medicaid Budget and Expenditure System. CMS collects managed care expenditures on specific lines of the CMS-64 form.

[10] To analyze trends over time, expenditures were adjusted for inflation using the gross domestic product price index to 2014 dollars. Under comprehensive risk based managed care, MCOs cover all or most Medicaid-covered services for beneficiaries and are at financial risk if

spending on benefits and administration exceeds capitation payments from the state, which provide a set amount of payment per beneficiary per month.

[11] With the exception of Michigan, the state fiscal year 2014 for the selected states runs from July 2013 through June 2014. Michigan's state fiscal year 2014 is from October 2013 through September 2014.

[12] Six of our eight states had one auto assignment methodology, while the other two states, Arizona and Florida, had separate auto assignment methodologies for two groups of beneficiaries. Arizona had separate methodologies for acute care and long-term care beneficiaries, and Florida had separate auto assignment methodologies for its Managed Medical Assistance Standard and MediKids beneficiaries. Unless otherwise specified, references to Arizona and Florida refer to the acute or standard beneficiaries.

[13] We defined beneficiary-related factors to include factors such as: (1) prior beneficiary relationship with a plan or provider, (2) current family plan or provider, or (3) enrollment in related plans, such as an affiliated long-term care plan. We considered a state to have beneficiary factors as part of its auto assignment methods if the factors were included in the auto assignment documentation or relevant section of the state managed care contract (typically the enrollment section). For example, Louisiana specifically included prior plan relationships and other beneficiary factors in its auto assignment documentation, while Michigan addressed beneficiary factors through contract enrollment policies.

[14] Under FFS, Medicaid pays providers for each service provided to a Medicaid beneficiary.

[15] Between July 2013 and December 2014, the number of states using managed care increased from 37 to 39.

[16] States may provide the services they carve out of their managed care contract to beneficiaries either through FFS or in another type of managed care program.

[17] The level of state discretion depends on the legal authority under which the state is operating the program.

[18] In general, states use actuarial accounting firms to certify their annual MCO payment rates. States use either previous Medicaid MCO encounter data or claims data from the Medicaid FFS population as data sources to develop the rates. States build a certain percentage for administrative expenses and profit into the rates.

[19] Insurance offered by large employers is known as large group insurance. Federal law defines a large employer as having an average of 51 or more employees during the preceding calendar year; however, states may apply this definition based on an average of 101 or more employees. See 42 U.S.C. §§ 300gg-91(e), 18024(b).

MA is the private plan alternative to the traditional Medicare FFS program. CMS contracts with MA organizations to provide covered services to beneficiaries who enroll in one of their plans. Under Medicare Part D, prescription drug plan sponsors—including private health insurers—contract with CMS to provide a voluntary outpatient prescription drug benefit for Medicare beneficiaries.

[20] Insurance purchased by individuals in a non-group setting is individual insurance. Insurance offered by small employers is known as small group insurance. Federal law defines a small employer as having an average of 1 to 50 employees during the preceding calendar year; however, states may apply this definition based on an average of 1 to 100 employees. See 42 U.S.C. §§ 300gg-91(e), 18024(b).

[21] Private Insurers: Pub. L. No. 111-148, §§ 1001(5), 10101(f), 124 Stat. 136, 885 (codified at 42 U.S.C. 300gg-18(b)(1)(A)), 45 C.F.R. §§ 158.101 et seq. (2014); MA organizations: 42 C.F.R. § 422.2400 et seq. (2014); Part D sponsors: 42 C.F.R. § 423.2400 et seq. (2014).

[22] MA organizations and Medicare Part D plan sponsors must also account for direct benefits to beneficiaries in the form of reductions, if any, of Medicare Part B premiums. Specifically, the MLR for MA organizations and Part D plan sponsors is expressed as the percentage of total revenue (less state and federal taxes, and licensing and regulatory fees) that is spent on medical claims, quality improvement activities, and any direct benefits to beneficiaries in the form of reduced Medicare Part B premiums.

[23] See 45 C.F.R. §§ 158.150(b), 158.151 (2014).

[24] In our previous work on the implementation of MLR requirements, we found that private insurers paid about $1.1 billion in total rebates to enrollees and policyholders who paid premiums in 2011, the first year that insurers were subject to the PPACA MLR requirements, and about $520 million in rebates in 2012. See GAO, *Private Health Insurance: Early Effects of Medical Loss Ratio Requirements and Rebates on Insurers and Enrollees,* GAO-14-580 (Washington, D.C.: July 10, 2014).

[25] The rebates for private plans and the remittances for MA organizations and Part D plans are determined by taking the difference between the applicable PPACA MLR standard and the insurer's actual MLR and multiplying it by the insurer's premiums, after federal and state taxes, and licensing or regulatory fees are removed.

[26] Under CMS's proposed rule, if the state requires MCOs to meet an MLR minimum, that minimum would have to be 85 percent or higher. In addition, CMS's proposed rule would require states to ensure that MCOs calculate and report MLRs annually, and that the reported MLRs are taken into account in the rate setting process and rates would be set such that MCOs can reasonably achieve an MLR of at least 85 percent.

[27] See 42 C.F.R. § 438.50(f) (2014). An "existing provider-beneficiary relationship" is one in which the provider was the main source of Medicaid services for the beneficiary during the previous year.

[28] These numbers reflect federal expenditures for comprehensive, risk-based managed care reported by all states and the District of Columbia. Combined federal and state spending for managed care in fiscal year 2014 totaled $170 billion.

[29] For this analysis, expenditures were adjusted for inflation using the gross domestic product price index to 2014 dollars. The proportion of federal expenditures for managed care in fiscal year 2014 was slightly higher than the proportion of state expenditures for that purpose—38 percent and 34 percent, respectively. Expenditures for managed care in 2014 represented 36 percent of total, combined federal and state Medicaid expenditures.

[30] The federal government matches state expenditures for Medicaid services on the basis of a statutory formula based, in part, on a state's per capita income. Federal law specifies that this federal match may range from 50 to 83 percent. For states that expand Medicaid, the federal government will pay an enhanced match—100 percent of the cost of covering newly eligible enrollees—in 2014, 2015, and 2016, with the federal match gradually reduced to 90 percent by 2020.

[31] See Department of Health and Human Services, Centers for Medicare & Medicaid Services, Office of the Actuary, *2014 Actuarial Report on the Financial Outlook for Medicaid* (Washington, D.C.: 2015).

[32] Differences in the federal matching rate, which can range from 50 to 83 percent, may have contributed to this variation.

[33] Capitation payments include both the state and federal share of the cost, as applicable.

[34] These numbers reflect the average payment per full year equivalent, which represents 12 months of enrollment.

[35] CMS data indicated that 14 of the 37 states with managed care as of July 2013 enrolled individuals requiring LTSS.

[36] CMS data indicated that of the 37 states with managed care as of July 2013, 3 provided LTSS separately, 13 provided behavioral health services separately, 5 provided dental services separately, and 10 provided transportation services separately.

[37] For the state with the lowest rate, rates were for calendar year 2013. For the state with the highest rate, the rates were for calendar year 2015. For the two remaining states, rates were for contract year and state fiscal year 2014, respectively.

[38] For the state with the lowest rate, rates were for the contract year beginning in February 2015. For the state with the highest rate, the rates were for July through December of 2014. For the two remaining states, rates were for contract year and state fiscal year 2014, respectively.

[39] See GAO, *Medicaid: Service Utilization Patterns for Beneficiaries in Managed Care,* GAO-15-481 (Washington, D.C.: May 29, 2015) and *Medicaid Payment: Comparisons of Selected Services under Fee-for-Service, Managed Care, and Private Insurance,* GAO-14-533 (Washington, D.C.: July 15, 2014).

[40] While not an MLR minimum, Washington applies an MLR risk corridor of 86 to 92 percent to MCOs that is specific to the adult expansion population. This risk corridor represents the range of MLRs that the state ensures is maintained for the adult expansion population covered by MCOs. If an MCO has an MLR for this population that is below 86 percent it must refund a certain proportion of funds to the state. If it has an MLR that is above 92 percent, the state will pay additional funds to the MCO up to a defined threshold.

[41] As previously noted, under CMS's proposed rule, if the state requires MCOs to meet an MLR minimum, that minimum would have to be 85 percent or higher. In addition, CMS's proposed rule would require states to ensure that MCOs calculate and report MLRs annually, that the reported MLRs are taken into account in the rate setting process, and that rates would be set such that MCOs can reasonably achieve an MLR of at least 85 percent.

[42] In its proposed rule, CMS would require that MCOs annually submit a report to states containing pertinent information for calculating the MLR. These elements would be reconciled with the audited financial reports that CMS also proposes that plans submit to states annually.

[43] If an MCO has an MLR for its expansion population that is below 85 percent it must pay the state the difference between 85 percent of total net capitation payments to the MCO and the actual allowed medical expenses incurred for that region. If an MCO has an MLR for its adult expansion population that is above 95 percent, then the state will pay the MCO the difference between the MCO's allowed medical expenses and 95 percent of net capitation payments received for that region. Pennsylvania is planning to implement a similar MLR risk corridor policy in 2015.

[44] GAO-14-580.

[45] The preamble to CMS's proposed rule encourages, but would not require, states to use remittances as an incentive for MCOs to comply with a state MLR requirement if implemented.

[46] Under CMS's proposed rule, rates must be set to allow MCOs to account for a reasonable amount of administrative costs. In the preamble, CMS explained that in addition to setting rates such that MCOs are allowed to reasonably achieve an MLR of at least 85 percent, states should set rates so that MLRs do not exceed a reasonable maximum threshold to account for reasonable administrative costs.

[47] Overall program goals were generally considered after plan performance factors in the four states that considered such factors.

[48] Arizona, California, Florida, Louisiana, Michigan, Pennsylvania, and Washington reported that they tracked these rates, generally for state fiscal year 2014. Tennessee officials told us that the state does not track auto assignment rates, although they estimated that the auto assignment rate would be quite high.

[49] Washington officials estimated that approximately 1 to 3 percent of beneficiaries switched plans. State officials told us that the state changed its policy in May 2015 to give its Medicaid beneficiaries time to choose a plan before being auto assigned to a state-selected managed care plan. Other states in our sample reported that beneficiaries could switch plans within a range of 30 to 90 days, depending on the state.

[50] While eligible beneficiaries are selecting a plan, they may be enrolled in FFS or managed care. Florida officials told us the state plans to phase out the time period where beneficiaries are covered by FFS. Beneficiaries would still have a chance to choose their plan, but the state would enroll them in plans more quickly.

[51] CMS's proposed rule would also make changes to state auto assignment methods, for example, by specifying additional factors that states may take into account when auto assigning.

End Notes for Appendix III

[1] 42 C.F.R. § 438.702 (2014).

[2] Arizona's, Louisiana's, and Michigan's contracts indicated that performance incentives may be financed by withholding a certain percentage of the capitation payment made to each MCO. Arizona and Louisiana withhold 1 and 2 percent of the monthly capitation payment, respectively, while Michigan withholds less than 1 percent annually.

[3] However, officials from one state told us that accreditation expenses can be incorporated into the payment rates, and, as such, be a part of the costs that the state and federal government incur to fund the program.

[4] 42 C.F.R. § 438.202(e) (2014).

[5] Under the proposed rule, all states would need to update their quality strategies because CMS is also proposing that the quality strategy documents cover their entire Medicaid program, not just the managed care portions. As such, states that did not previously submit quality strategy documents because they did not offer managed care in their Medicaid programs would need to submit a quality strategy document for their overall Medicaid program to CMS. Furthermore, CMS has proposed to change the method through which the quality strategies are submitted. Instead of requiring states to send the agency the quality strategy, CMS is proposing that states make them available to the agency and the public via their Medicaid websites.

[6] If these states had not made significant changes to their strategies, then no updated copies would have been required. According to agency officials, two of these states submitted draft quality statement documents to CMS in 2014; however, they have yet to submit finalized versions.

[7] 42 U.S.C. § 1396u-2(c)(2); 42 C.F.R. § 438.350(a) (2014).

In: Medicaid Managed Care
Editor: Geneva Barrett
ISBN: 978-1-63485-817-5

Chapter 2

MEDICAID PROGRAM INTEGRITY: IMPROVED GUIDANCE NEEDED TO BETTER SUPPORT EFFORTS TO SCREEN MANAGED CARE PROVIDERS*

United States Government Accountability Office

WHY GAO DID THIS STUDY

GAO has reported that Medicaid remains a high-risk program, partly due to concerns about improper payments. Screening of providers is important to help prevent improper payments. Under managed care, states contract with plans to provide services to beneficiaries.

GAO was asked to examine the screening of managed care providers. GAO examined (1) states' and plans' experiences using federal databases to screen providers; and (2) how states and plans share data about ineligible providers. GAO interviewed officials from 10 states, selected generally based on enrollment and geography, and representatives from 16 plans from among these states. GAO reviewed those states' Medicaid program websites and plan contracts, and relevant federal laws, regulations, and guidance; and interviewed officials from CMS and the Department of Health and Human Services' Office of Inspector General.

* This is an edited, reformatted and augmented version of a United States Government Accountability Office, Publication No. GAO-16-402, dated April 2016.

What GAO Recommends

GAO recommends that CMS (1) consider additional databases used in screening, (2) collaborate with the Social Security Administration to improve access to the Death Master File, (3) coordinate with other agencies to develop a common identifier across databases, and (4) provide state Medicaid programs with guidance that establishes expectations and best practices on sharing provider screening data among states and plans. HHS concurred with our recommendations.

What GAO Found

GAO found that the selected states and Medicaid managed care plans face significant challenges in screening providers for eligibility to participate in the Medicaid program. Based on information we received from two selected states and 16 selected plans, GAO found that the states and plans used information that was fragmented across 22 databases managed by 15 different federal agencies to screen providers. These databases included databases that the Centers for Medicare & Medicaid Services (CMS) had not identified for use in screening providers. Officials from some states noted that these additional databases provided better assurance they would not enroll ineligible providers— i.e., providers who have been barred from participating in federal health care programs. Federal internal control standards stress the importance of collecting quality information to achieve objectives and assess risks. However, the variety of databases used for screening purposes beyond those identified by CMS, along with the current rate of improper payments to Medicaid providers, suggests that CMS might not have identified all reliable sources of information about ineligible providers that could help states and plans achieve program objectives. State officials and plan representatives also said that accessing and using fragmented information from multiple and disparate federal databases challenged their screening efforts. For example, they reported difficulties accessing certain databases, such as the Social Security Administration's Death Master File, and conducting and confirming identified provider matches across databases, particularly those not based on a unique national provider identifier. CMS has not coordinated with other agencies to address these challenges. Federal internal control standards state that agencies should use quality data that are complete, current, accurate, and accessible—and have a logical connection to the program—to achieve agency goals to reduce fraud. However, the difficulties states and plans experienced accessing databases and confirming matches could result in provider screening efforts that do not ensure that ineligible providers are accurately and consistently identified.

GAO also found that the selected states reviewed used inconsistent practices to make data on ineligible providers publicly available. States must ensure that none of their providers has been determined to be ineligible anywhere in the United States. Although CMS has issued guidance encouraging states to share data on ineligible providers through its Medicaid provider termination notification system, doing so is optional, not all states are using the list, and it is not available to Medicaid managed care plans. Moreover, CMS has not provided states with guidance on other ways to share their data on ineligible providers or how to access other states' data on ineligible providers. The 10 states GAO selected varied in how they shared data on ineligible providers. Plans are not required to make their own data on ineligible providers publicly available, and the 16 selected plans shared their data with states at differing intervals and, in rare cases, with other plans. The inconsistency with which this information is shared across states and plans creates the potential that providers could be ineligible in some states while still receiving payments from Medicaid in other states.

ABBREVIATIONS

CMS	Centers for Medicare & Medicaid Services
DEA	Drug Enforcement Administration
DMF	Death Master File
EAR	Export Administration Regulations
EPLS	Excluded Parties List System
FEHBP	Federal Employees Health Benefits Program
FFS	fee for service
GSA	General Services Administration
HCERA	Health Care and Education Reconciliation Act of 2010
HHS	Department of Health and Human Services
HHS-OIG	Department of Health and Human Services Office of Inspector General
LEIE	List of Excluded Individuals and Entities
MED	Medicare Exclusion Database

MMC	Medicaid managed care
NPI	National Provider Identifier
NCQA	National Committee for Quality Assurance
NPDB	National Practitioner Data Bank
NPPES	National Plan and Provider Enumeration System
OPM	Office of Personnel Management
PACER	Public Access to Court Electronic Records
PECOS	Provider Enrollment Chain and Ownership System
PPACA	Patient Protection and Affordable Care Act
SAM	System for Award Management
SSA	Social Security Administration
TIN	Taxpayer Identification Number

* * *

April 22, 2016

The Honorable Thomas R. Carper
Ranking Member
Committee on Homeland Security and Governmental Affairs
United States Senate

Dear Senator Carper:

The Medicaid program financed health care coverage for an estimated 69 million beneficiaries with estimated expenditures of $529 billion in fiscal year 2015.[1] This federal-state health care program for low-income and medically needy individuals finances the delivery of health care services to beneficiaries through fee-for-service (FFS) payments to participating providers and capitated payments to Medicaid managed care (MMC) plans under the terms of their contracts with the state. Under the managed care delivery model, states typically contract with MMC plans to provide a specific set of Medicaid-covered services to beneficiaries and pay the MMC plans a set amount per beneficiary per month—referred to as capitation payments—to provide those services. The Centers for Medicare & Medicaid Services (CMS), within the Department of Health and Human Services (HHS), is responsible for broad oversight of the Medicaid program, while states are responsible for the daily administration of their individual Medicaid programs, including program integrity activities. In its broad oversight role, CMS develops guidance and provides assistance to the states in administering their Medicaid programs. In February 2015, we reported that Medicaid remains a high-risk program because of concerns about the adequacy of fiscal oversight, including improper payments to Medicaid providers.[2] CMS estimated that $29.12 billion, or 9.78 percent, of federal Medicaid expenditures for fiscal year 2015 were improper payments.[3]

Because provider actions can be a major factor behind improper payments, the integrity of the Medicaid program depends, in large part, on ensuring that only eligible providers participate in the program. Consequently, screening providers is important in helping prevent improper payments, including fraud and abuse. In 2000, we raised concerns about the effectiveness of states' screening and enrollment processes in preventing potentially fraudulent providers from enrolling in the Medicaid program.[4] More recently, we examined approximately 881,000 Medicaid providers in four states and found that in fiscal year 2011 hundreds of these providers were potentially receiving improper Medicaid payments. The providers had suspended or revoked medical licenses, had invalid addresses, were identified as deceased in federal death files, or had been excluded from federal health care programs, including Medicaid.[5] Our prior work has also concluded that comprehensive state screening and enrollment processes that prevent fraudulent providers from billing Medicaid are more efficient in protecting Medicaid funds than attempting to recover these funds once payments have been made.[6] For the purposes of this report, an "ineligible or potentially ineligible provider" means a provider who has been, or could be, excluded by HHS's Office of Inspector General (HHS-OIG) or terminated by a state from participating in Medicaid under any applicable requirements.

As states move their Medicaid programs to managed care, the screening of MMC plan providers becomes increasingly important and increasingly complex. As of July 2013, the date of the most recent enrollment data available, about 55 percent of total Medicaid enrollment was in managed care, a percentage that has likely grown since.[7] In addition, MMC expenditures are growing at a faster rate than FFS expenditures because of the Medicaid expansions under the Patient Protection and Affordable Care Act (PPACA).[8] Further, the HHS-OIG has noted the emergence of MMC fraud, citing the increase in the agency's workload on MMC fraud cases, some of which resulted in inflated payments to MMC plans. The flexibility states have in setting up their Medicaid programs—in the case of screening MMC plan providers, states either screen providers, or they delegate screening to plans, or use a combination of both approaches— makes identifying ineligible providers across multiple states a complex task. According to a 2016 estimate by the Congressional Budget Office, managed care providers who have been determined to be ineligible for the Medicaid program, but continue to participate, receive $3 million in federal Medicaid payments annually.

You asked us to examine the availability and use of databases and information necessary to screen MMC plan providers. This report examines

1. selected states' and MMC plans' experiences using federal databases to screen providers; and
2. how states and MMC plans share data about ineligible providers.

To obtain information on the federal databases that states and MMC plans use to screen providers and their experiences using these databases, we first selected 10 states—California, Florida, Illinois, Minnesota, Missouri, New Jersey, New York, Tennessee, Texas, and Washington—generally based on MMC beneficiary enrollment and geographic distribution. We contacted Medicaid program officials in these states to discuss whether the state or the MMC plans primarily screen MMC plan providers. We determined that 2 states conduct their own provider screening and 8 states primarily delegate provider screening to MMC plans. We then contacted state Medicaid officials in the two states that primarily screen providers, and representatives from the 16 plans in states where plans primarily screen providers. We discussed which federal databases they use to screen providers in order to help prevent ineligible providers from enrolling and their experiences with using the databases. The experiences of the Medicaid officials in the selected states and the representatives in the selected MMC plans are not generalizable to all plans in the states or to other states. In addition, we reviewed applicable federal laws and regulations; CMS reviews of state program integrity activities; CMS guidance on database use for the screening of MMC plan providers; and Medicaid managed care contracts in the 10 states. Further, we evaluated the sufficiency of CMS guidance related to provider screening against our fraud prevention framework and relevant federal internal control standards.[9] Finally, we interviewed CMS and HHS-OIG officials to obtain information about their databases, and obtained and reviewed documentation on the various federal databases identified by the states and plans.

To obtain information about how states and MMC plans share information and data on ineligible providers with other MMC plans and states, we contacted Medicaid officials in all 10 selected states and plan representatives from the 16 selected plans. In addition, we searched the Medicaid program websites in each of the 10 states to determine whether state data on terminated providers were publicly available; the type of information provided; and the ease of searching, finding, and downloading state information. The experiences of the Medicaid officials in the selected states and the representatives in the selected MMC plans are not generalizable to all plans in the states or to other states. We also reviewed CMS guidance on sharing data regarding these providers and relevant federal internal control standards.

We conducted this performance audit from March 2015 to April 2016 in accordance with generally accepted government auditing standards. Those standards require that we plan and perform the audit to obtain sufficient, appropriate evidence to provide a reasonable basis for our findings and conclusions based on our audit objectives. We believe that the evidence obtained provides a reasonable basis for our findings and conclusions based on our audit objectives.

BACKGROUND

Federal laws require both state and federal entities to protect the Medicaid program from fraud, waste, and abuse. States have primary responsibility for reducing, identifying, and recovering improper payments. Federal entities typically provide oversight, guidance, and program and law enforcement support.

States' program integrity activities include a screening process to help ensure that ineligible providers do not participate in the Medicaid program. Federal regulations establish screening requirements that apply when states enroll FFS providers into their Medicaid program. Because states are required to enroll FFS providers, but have discretion on whether to enroll MMC plan providers, MMC plan providers would not be subject to the same screening requirements as FFS providers unless the state opted to enroll them.[10] States that do not enroll MMC plan providers have flexibility in how they screen them.[11] This occurs when states require the MMC plans to screen and enroll providers directly into their networks by delegating these responsibilities to the plans in their contracts. In past work, we concluded that states that maintain centralized control over the provider screening process and require MMC plan providers to enroll with the state Medicaid agency may be better positioned to ensure the integrity of their Medicaid programs.[12]

Federal health programs, including Medicaid, are prohibited from paying for any items or services rendered by an ineligible provider. The HHSOIG determines which providers are excluded from the federal health programs, and thus ineligible, and maintains the List of Excluded Individuals and Entities (LEIE).[13] Grounds for exclusion include convictions for program-related fraud and patient abuse, and suspension or revocation of a medical license for reasons bearing on professional competence or performance. While states may delegate provider screening to the MMC plans, the states remain responsible for ensuring that they do not pay ineligible providers for Medicaid health care items and services. CMS is prohibited by federal law from making payments to states for any amount expended for items or services provided by an ineligible provider.[14] Any such payments constitute overpayments and are therefore subject to recoupment. In addition, civil monetary penalties may be imposed against MMC plans that employ or enter into contracts with ineligible providers.

Further, PPACA and its implementing regulations require state Medicaid agencies to terminate the participation of any provider that has been terminated on or after January 1, 2011, under Medicare or under any other state Medicaid program or Children's Health Insurance Program.[15] CMS defines termination to mean that a state Medicaid program, Children's Health Insurance Program, or the Medicare program has taken action to revoke a provider's billing privileges for cause, and the provider has exhausted all applicable appeal rights or the timeline for appeal has expired.[16] A termination for cause may include, but is not limited to, terminations based upon fraud, integrity, or quality issues.[17] Prior to PPACA, if one state terminated a provider from its Medicaid program, the provider could potentially enroll in or continue participation in another state's Medicaid program, leaving the latter state's program vulnerable to potential fraud, waste, and abuse. In response to the PPACA requirement for CMS to establish a process for sharing information about terminated providers with state agencies, CMS established a web-based portal—the Medicaid provider termination notification system—where CMS and state Medicaid agencies can submit information about providers that meet CMS's criteria for having been terminated for cause from Medicare, Medicaid, or the Children's Health Insurance Program. However, according to CMS officials, states' use of this portal to report terminations is voluntary.

In response to PPACA's requirement to establish procedures for screening providers, CMS issued regulations that set forth minimum requirements applicable to the screening of Medicaid FFS providers, although states have flexibility to establish more stringent screening requirements.[18] Among other requirements, CMS designated four federal databases that states must use to screen providers: (1) the Social Security Administration's (SSA) Death Master File (DMF), (2) HHS's National Plan and Provider Enumeration System (NPPES), (3) the LEIE, and (4) the Excluded Parties List System (EPLS) maintained by the General Services Administration.[19] In December 2014, CMS issued guidance to assist states when conducting required federal database checks on FFS providers.[20] In the guidance, CMS noted that MMC plans are not mandated by regulation to screen providers who enroll in their networks. However, CMS stated that it considered the requirements under its regulation to be program safeguards that would be prudent in managed care settings. CMS also noted that states may delegate these requirements to their MMC plans through their contracts with them. In guidance issued to MMC plans, CMS recommended that plans use the LEIE and EPLS to identify ineligible providers.[21]

Selected States and Medicaid Managed Care Plans Face Significant Challenges Screening Providers

According to two selected states and 16 selected MMC plans that screen MMC plan providers, their efforts are challenged by fragmented information and difficulty accessing and using particular databases.

Efforts to Screen Providers Are Based on Information that Is Fragmented across Multiple and Disparate Federal Databases

According to the two selected state officials and 16 selected MMC plan representatives we contacted, the information they use to screen MMC plan providers is fragmented across multiple and disparate federal databases. Overall, these two selected states and 16 selected plans identified a total of 22 databases managed by 15 different federal agencies. Representatives from 13 of the 16 plans reported using between 5 and 8 of these federal databases, while officials from the two states that directly screen managed care providers reported using 5 and 6 databases. Table 1 lists the 22 databases that these selected state officials and plan representatives said they used in their screening of MMC plan providers, the agencies that managed them, and the role the databases play in the screening of providers. (See appendix I for additional details on each of these federal databases.)

Table 1. Federal Databases Identified by Two Selected States and 16 Selected Medicaid Managed Care (MMC) Plans for Screening MMC Plan Providers

		Entity conducting screening	
Managing agency and database	Use in screening providers	States (2)	Plans in8 states (16)
Department of Health and Human Services (HHS) Office of Inspector General (HHS-OIG)			
List of Excluded Individuals and Entities (LEIE)[a]	Identifies providers that the HHS-OIG has excluded from participation in federal health care programs.	2	16
OIG Most Wanted Fugitives	Identifies providers who are on HHS-OIG's list of most wanted health care fugitives.	0	2
HHS Centers for Medicare & Medicaid Services (CMS)			
Medicare Exclusions Database	Provides information on excluded providers and is CMS's equivalent to HHS-OIG's LEIE.	2	11
Medicare Opt-out	Lists providers who voluntarily request, and are permitted, to opt-out of the Medicare program.	0	3
National Plan & Provider Enumeration System (NPPES)[a]	Contains a directory of providers with active National Provider Identifiers.[b]	2	16
Provider Enrollment, Chain and Ownership System (PECOS)	Is an Internet-based system to which Medicare providers submit and update their enrollment data. States use PECOS to obtain information on whether providers are eligible to participate in Medicare and Medicaid.	2	0[c]
HHS Health Resources and Services Administration			
National Practitioner Data Bank (NPDB)	Among other things, identifies health care providers who have been disciplined by a state licensing board, professional society, or health care provider, or have been named in a medical malpractice settlement or judgment.	0	16

		Entity conducting screening	
Managing agency and database	Use in screening providers	States (2)	Plans in8 states (16)
Department of Commerce, Bureau of Industry and Security			
Denied Persons List	Identifies individuals and entities that have been denied export privileges by written order to the Department of Commerce.	0	1
Entity List	Identifies foreign parties that are subject to specific license requirements for the export, re-export and/or transfer (in-country) of specific items.	0	1
Unverified List	Identifies parties that are ineligible to receive items subject to the Export Administration Regulations by means of a license exception.	0	1
Department of Justice, Drug Enforcement Administration (DEA)			
Administrative Actions Against Registrants	Identifies those providers registered with the DEA, against whom the agency has taken administrative action.	0	1
DEA Number	Provides proof of providers' DEA registration number.	0	2
Department of State			
Designated Foreign Terrorist Organizations	Lists foreign organizations that are designated by the Secretary of State as Foreign Terrorist Organizations, in accordance of section 219 of the Immigration and Nationality Act, as amended.	0	1
Department of Treasury, Office of Assets Control			
Specially Designated Nationals List	Identifies those providers whose assets are blocked and with whom U.S. entities are generally prohibited from dealing.	0	5[d]
Federal Bureau of Investigation			
Wanted Fugitives	Provides a list of Federal Bureau of Investigation fugitives.	0	1
Federal Judiciary			
Public Access to Court Electronic Records (PACER)	Is a centralized, electronic public access service, provided by the federal judiciary, which allows users to obtain case and docket information online from federal appellate, district, and bankruptcy courts, and the PACER Case Locator.	0	1

Table 1. (Continued)

		Entity conducting screening	
Managing agency and database	Use in screening providers	States (2)	Plans in8 states (16)
Federal Financial Institutions Examination Council			
Politically Exposed Persons	Lists current or former senior foreign political figures, their immediate family, and their close associates, who potentially pose a risk that their funds may be the proceeds of foreign corruption.	0	1
General Services Administration			
Excluded Parties List System (EPLS)/System for Award Management (SAM)[a,e]	Identifies parties that have been suspended or debarred from receiving a wide range of federal funds.	2	16
Internal Revenue Service			
Taxpayer Identification Number Matching	Allows authorized users to match taxpayer identification numbers with names.	0	1
Office of Personnel Management			
Federal Employees Health Benefits Program Administrative Sanctions	Lists providers who have been suspended and debarred by the Office of Personnel Management's Office of Inspector General because they have, among other things, lost professional licenses, violated provisions of a federal program, been debarred by another federal agency, or been convicted of a crime related to delivery of or payment for health care services.	0	1
Social Security Administration			
Death Master File[a]	Identifies Social Security number holders who are deceased.	1[f]	14[g]
United States Postal Service			
Look Up A Zip Code	Allows zip code searches by address, city, and state.	0	1

Source: GAO analysis of information from the two selected states that conduct the screening of MMC plan providers and 16 selected plans . | GAO-16-402

Notes: According to information we obtained from Medicaid program officials in each of the 10 selected states, 2 of these states conduct the screening of MMC plan providers. In the other 8 states, the MMC plans are primarily responsible for this screening.

In these 8 states, we obtained information from representatives from each of the two MMC plans with the most Medicaid beneficiaries.

[a]CMS regulations require state Medicaid agencies to use this federal database when screening fee-for-service providers. 42 C.F.R. § 455.436 (2015).

[b]The National Provider Identifier (NPI) is a national, unique 10-digit identification number assigned to health care providers that CMS specified must be used in specified administrative and financial transactions for its health care providers and suppliers, in accordance with the Health Insurance Portability and Accountability Act.

[c]As of February 2016, this database is only available to states, not to plans.

[d]Representatives from one plan told us that in addition to the Specially Designated Individuals list, they use another five related Office of Foreign Assets Control databases that generally focus on U.S. sanctions against specific countries.

[e]In July 2012, the General Services Administration migrated the Excluded Parties List System (EPLS) into the System for Award Management, a comprehensive database that combines a number of federal procurement data sources, including EPLS.

[f]Officials from the state that did not use the Death Master File at the time of our review told us that they were in the process of procuring a subscription for it.

[g]Representatives from one plan that did not use the Death Master File at the time of our review told us that they intend to use it in the future.

According to state Medicaid officials in the two selected states that do their own screening of providers, both states used the LEIE, EPLS, and NPPES, and one also used the DMF.[22] In addition, both states checked CMS's Medicare Exclusions Database and its Provider Enrollment, Chain and Ownership System (PECOS).

Almost all of the selected MMC plans reported using three databases—NPPES, DMF, and HHS's National Practitioner Data Bank—in addition to the two databases recommended by CMS guidance. Plans also reported using several other of the federal databases identified in table 1. Officials from some states noted that plans checking more databases than recommended by CMS provided better assurance they would not enroll ineligible providers and helped provide a more comprehensive background on a provider. For example, by checking federal databases beyond the two recommended by CMS for MMC plans (LEIE and EPLS), plans may find background on a provider's termination or identify a past administrative action taken against the provider by the Drug Enforcement Administration. However, this also means that provider screenings within a state may not always be conducted consistently, as the additional databases checked may vary by plan.

Additionally, all 10 selected states use the health plan accreditation requirements of the National Committee for Quality Assurance (NCQA) in their monitoring of state MMC plans, because it includes provider screening guidelines, such as assessing providers' practice history, verifying their credentials, education, training, malpractice history and disciplinary actions, and monitoring providers' sanctions, complaints, and quality issues. Half of the states require that their plans be accredited by NCQA, and the rest recognize NCQA accreditation as compliance with federal guidance for screening MMC plan providers. In particular, to meet the NCQA accreditation requirements, plans need to obtain information beyond what the LEIE and EPLS provide. For example, to meet NCQA's requirement that they verify provider history and other disciplinary actions, plans must check the National Practitioners' Data Bank, a large central federal data bank of all reports made against all health care professionals, including fraud, abuse, licensure actions, or malpractice reports.

Federal internal control standards stress the importance of collecting quality information to achieve objectives and assess risks. To do this, the standards state that it is necessary to identify information requirements and use data from reliable sources. [23] However, the variety of databases checked by states and MMC plans beyond those specified by CMS, the use of NCQA's accreditation requirements in all 10 states, along with the current rate of improper payments to Medicaid providers, suggests that CMS might not have identified all reliable sources of information about ineligible providers. This makes it difficult for the states and MMC plans to achieve the Medicaid program's objectives. Moreover, the variety of databases that the states and MMC plans have chosen to check raises the possibility that they might be using information of varying quality to screen providers. All of the states and MMC plans that screened providers checked more databases than are currently specified by CMS for this purpose, but CMS has not assessed whether there are benefits to checking the additional databases. Without an assessment of these additional databases and their potential contribution to improving the effectiveness of screening providers, and ultimately reducing improper Medicaid payments, CMS cannot be certain that states and MMC plans are using information of sufficient quality to screen providers.

Screening Efforts Are Hampered by Difficulties Accessing and Using Databases

State Medicaid officials and MMC plan representatives said that accessing and using information that is fragmented across multiple and disparate federal databases hampered them in their efforts to screen providers. CMS has not collaborated with other agencies to explore options for enhancing the ability of states and plans to access and use comprehensive information during the screening process, including information about deceased providers, and thus better ensure that ineligible or potentially fraudulent providers do not bill Medicaid.

Accessing Particular Databases

State officials and plan representatives noted problems accessing two specific databases. Officials from one state and representatives from one plan identified cost as a challenge to using the DMF, which is only available with a paid subscription.[24] CMS officials told us that they are interested in collaborating with SSA to facilitate sharing DMF data with states. Additionally, representatives from one plan said that having access to PECOS—a CMS database currently unavailable to plans— would help improve their screening process because it would help corroborate information from providers.

Representatives from two plans said that they experienced challenges obtaining assistance when they had general problems using federal databases. For example, representatives from one plan said that it could be difficult to identify an individual at a federal agency who could not only assist them, but also who understands Medicaid. Plan officials said that if they were able to contact someone, the agency might be hesitant to provide the plan with additional information about a provider termination, because MMC plans are not government entities.

Confirming Identified Matches

Representatives from seven selected plans said that the technical process of conducting the matches and confirming identified matches was challenging. For example, some plan representatives said they check the eligibility status of thousands of providers at regular intervals, typically monthly, and said that these checks can be particularly challenging if the database does not allow the user to compare multiple provider names at one time.

Plan representatives said that confirming the accuracy of identified matches was also challenging, because some databases contained limited provider data, particularly if a match is not based on a unique identifier, such as the national provider identifier (NPI). The lack of a consistent, unique identifier meant that it could be difficult to accurately match a potentially ineligible provider across databases.[25] Relying solely on basic information for matching, such as providers' names and addresses, can cause additional problems; for example, false positive matches for common names such as John Smith. In these instances, plans may have to take additional steps to confirm the match, such as contacting the provider or federal agency managing the database to obtain additional information that is not included in the database. Several plans told us that they would prefer to use the NPI to search the databases, because most providers are required to have an NPI. However, because NPI is a health-care specific unique identifier, it may not be used in databases external to HHS. Other unique identifiers that state officials and plan representatives suggested could be used across databases include Social Security numbers and taxpayer identification numbers, although the officials noted the sensitivity involved with using these numbers.

These challenges affect states' ability to ensure that only eligible providers in good standing participate in the Medicaid program. Federal internal control standards state that agencies should use quality data that are complete, current, accurate, and accessible, and have a logical connection to the program, such as the data regarding deceased individuals in the DMF, to achieve agency goals to reduce fraud.[26] Without consistent access to the DMF, states and plans risk paying deceased providers—a potential concern that we have identified in prior work.[27] The use of a consistent identifier would also help states and plans ensure that they are accurately identifying ineligible providers. However, CMS officials said they have not coordinated with other agencies to address these challenges. For example:

- Sharing CMS's DMF data: SSA officials told us that they recently received a request from CMS asking for permission to share DMF information with states and said that they are willing to work with CMS to develop a process to do so. CMS officials told us that they have had preliminary conversations with SSA and are interested in collaborating with SSA to develop a process to share the DMF with states. In addition to helping to ensure that states have access to DMF data and protecting the federal government from fraudulent payments to deceased providers, this arrangement could decrease federal and Medicaid expenditures. For example, SSA officials told us that in fiscal year 2014 CMS paid nearly $25,200 for the DMF data, including weekly updates, and states reported annual DMF subscription and implementation costs ranging from about $2,700 to

$67,000. Since one state and most of the plans reported using the DMF, CMS sharing its DMF subscription would likely produce state and federal savings for Medicaid.

- Collaborating with other agencies to use a unique identifier: CMS officials said that they have not considered collaborating with other agencies to explore using a unique identifier—such as the NPI—that would serve to improve the ability of states and plans to confirm the accuracy of matches across databases. Such collaboration could help to mitigate challenges experienced by states and MMC plans in confirming database matches efficiently and effectively, which potentially place federal dollars at risk for waste, fraud, and abuse.

Recent legislation has the potential to address some—but not all—of the challenges related to states' and health plans' use of federal databases. The Department of Treasury's Do Not Pay database is designed to reduce improper payments in federal programs and incorporates information from several of the federal databases states and plans use to screen providers. The Do Not Pay database is a source of centralized data that agencies must use to verify eligibility for federal payments and awards. The Do Not Pay database provides access to—among other data sources—EPLS, and the public version of the DMF. Officials from one state that delegates provider screenings to MMC plans said that having access to the Do Not Pay database would streamline their screening process. While the Do Not Pay database is currently only available to federal agencies, a recently enacted law will allow states and state contractors, including MMC plans, to access the database.[28] Other states and plans also indicated that a centralized database would be ideal, although they did not refer directly to the Do Not Pay database. CMS officials told us they are considering suggesting to states and plans that they use the Do Not Pay database for Medicaid managed care provider screening.

SELECTED STATES AND MEDICAID MANAGED CARE PLANS USE INCONSISTENT PRACTICES TO MAKE DATA ON INELIGIBLE PROVIDERS PUBLICLY AVAILABLE

States must ensure that none of their providers has been determined to be ineligible anywhere in the United States. CMS issued guidance in 2012 encouraging states to share data on ineligible providers through its Medicaid provider termination notification system; however, doing so is optional, not all states are using the list, and the list is not available to MMC plans.[29] In addition, CMS officials said they have not provided states with guidance on other ways to share their data on ineligible providers or how to access other states' data on ineligible providers.[30]

Our 10 selected states varied in how they shared data on ineligible providers, the location and usability of the data they shared, and the type of information they shared. All of our 10 selected states made data on their ineligible providers publicly available.[31] Specifically, they made their data available online, although they varied in where they posted these data on their websites and in the consistency of the information posted. For example, our review of the states' websites found that 5 states made the data available through their state's Office of Inspector General's website, while the 5 other states had these data on their Medicaid websites. Within these two groups, the data were sometimes displayed on a homepage and other times required users to click through a number of webpages to locate the data. All the states provided at least some export function as part of accessing their data on ineligible providers, which can facilitate the ease with which other states can access and use the information on the website. However, 2 states limited their data exports to PDF files, which have less search functionality than other formats like Microsoft Excel, which was used by the other 8 states. Eight of the selected states had a database search feature as part of their website and an export function, which allowed users to search for individual providers. Two websites allowed for verification of a Social Security number online. (See fig. 1.)

	State 1	State 2	State 3	State 4	State 5	State 6	State 7	State 8	State 9	State 10
Features										
Exportable Data	●	●	●	●	●	●	●	●	●	●
Database Search Feature	●	●	●	●	●	●	●	○	●	○
Social Security Number Verification Online	○	○	○	○	○	○	●	○	●	○

● Yes
○ No

Source: GAO. | GAO-16-402.

Figure 1. Usability Features on Publicly Available State Data on Ineligible Medicaid Providers from 10 Selected States.

The 10 selected states also varied in the types of data they made available about their ineligible providers. All 10 states included providers' first names, last names, and middle names or initials. Seven states included providers' NPI in their information on ineligible providers. Seven states included a category for a medical license number in their information on ineligible providers, but these data were not consistently presented across states. Four states included provider addresses, and seven states included provider type or specialty. One state included alias' that the ineligible providers might be using, and one state provided information on ineligible providers' affiliations with other provider groups or practices. (See fig. 2.)

	State 1	State 2	State 3	State 4	State 5	State 6	State 7	State 8	State 9	State 10
Last Name, First Name, and Middle Initial	●	●	●	●	●	●	●	●	●	●
Also Known As (AKA)/ Doing Business As (DBA) Names	●	○	○	○	○	○	○	○	○	○
Affiliations (Provider Groups)	○	○	●	○	○	○	○	○	○	○
Address(es)	●	○	●	●	○	●	○	○	○	○
Provider Type/ Specialty	●	●	●	●	●	○	●	○	●	○
National Provider Identifier (NPI)	●	●	○	○	●	●	●	●	●	○
License Number[a]	●	●	●	○	●	○	●	○	●	●

● Yes
○ No

Source: GAO. | GAO-16-402.

[a]The License Number field varied across states, with some states using a provider's state license number, while others used NPI.

Figure 2. Provider Identifiers for Publicly Available State Data on Ineligible Medicaid Providers from 10 Selected States.

	State 1	State 2	State 3	State 4	State 5	State 6	State 7	State 8	State 9	State 10
Exclusion Background										
Date of Exclusion	●	●	●	●	●	●	●	●	●	●
Action Type	○	●	●	○	○	●	●	○	○	●
Reason for Exclusion	○	●	○	○	●	●	●	●	●	○

● Yes
○ No

Source: GAO. | GAO-16-402.

Note: State data on ineligible Medicaid providers used a variety of action types, including but not limited to: "exclusion," "terminated," "voluntary withdrawal," "debarment," and "disqualification." For the purposes of this category, we are including all actions that appear on states' exclusion data.

Figure 3. Background Information on Publicly Available State Data on Ineligible Medicaid Providers from 10 Selected States.

The 10 states also varied in the information they provided about why providers became ineligible and in the terminology they used. All 10 states included the effective date providers became ineligible. Five states provided information on the action type that led to the provider becoming ineligible, which included, among other things, the terms “exclusion,” “terminated,” and “voluntary withdrawal.” While the HHS-OIG defines excluded providers as those providers it has determined to be ineligible for participation in federal health programs, states used varying terminology.[32] Six states also included the reason for the exclusion. (See fig. 3.)

Unlike states, MMC plans are not required to make their data on ineligible providers publicly available.[33] The 16 selected MMC plans reported sharing these data with their state Medicaid agencies at varying intervals and in rare cases, with other plans. Representatives from the 16 selected plans said they might share their data on ineligible providers with their states during periodic meetings that covered a variety of issues. However, the frequency and scope of these meetings varied. According to plan representatives, 1 plan met with the state at least monthly, 3 plans met with the state quarterly, 7 plans met with the state annually, and 3 plans met with the state biennially; officials from 1 plan said they met with the state frequently but did not provide a specific frequency for the meetings; and 1 plan did not provide this information. Representatives from the MMC plans said they generally did not share these data with other plans, with a few exceptions. For example, representatives from 1 plan said that they share information on ineligible providers with another plan they contract with in their state. Similarly, representatives from 3 MMC plans that were subsidiaries of large health care corporations with MMC plans in multiple states told us that they shared data on ineligible providers with the other plans in their networks. However, there is no process or requirement from CMS for them to share on a consistent basis.

Because states and MMC plans are prohibited from paying federal funds to providers that have been determined to be ineligible anywhere in the United States, sharing data on ineligible providers is an important control activity for preventing providers who are ineligible to participate in Medicaid in one state from enrolling in or billing Medicaid programs in other states. Federal internal control standards emphasize the importance of performing control activities routinely and consistently.[34] The inconsistency with which this information on ineligible providers is shared across states and MMC plans creates the potential that providers could be determined to be ineligible in some states, while still receiving payments from Medicaid in other states.

CONCLUSION

States and MMC plans rely on fragmented information from multiple and disparate databases to screen managed care providers to ensure that they are not paying providers determined to be ineligible to do business with the federal government. Currently, CMS guidance to states and MMC plans only touches upon a small subset of the 22 disparate databases that states and MMC plans check when screening providers, and does not provide information on what other databases would be helpful for screening providers. Because MMC plans we reviewed are using a variety of databases beyond those specified by CMS, it suggests that CMS might not have identified all reliable sources of information about ineligible providers that would be helpful to meet program objectives and assess risks. Without an assessment of these additional databases and their potential contribution to improving the effectiveness of screening providers, CMS cannot be certain that its guidance to states and MMC plans is comprehensive for screening providers.

States and plans have also been hampered in their efforts to access and use databases maintained by various federal agencies, because of differences in the characteristics of the databases, including difficulty accessing databases and conducting provider matches. CMS has not coordinated with other agencies to explore what options may exist to address these challenges.

CMS guidance on how states should share data on ineligible providers is also limited, resulting in significant inconsistency in how such information is shared across states. All 10 selected states made their data on ineligible providers publicly available, although they varied in where they posted the data on their websites and the consistency of the information posted. While all 10 states included providers' names, other data—such as NPI or other identifiers—were not consistently available. Anyone checking these data would be required to do additional work to confirm a provider match and state websites would require that the states conducting the screenings know how to locate the ineligible provider list. The inconsistency with which this information is shared across states and MMC plans creates the potential that providers could be determined to be ineligible in some states, while still receiving payments from Medicaid in other states.

RECOMMENDATIONS FOR EXECUTIVE ACTION

To improve the effectiveness of states' and plans' MMC plan provider screening efforts, we recommend that the Acting Administrator of CMS take the following three actions:

1. Consider which additional databases that states and MMC plans use to screen providers could be helpful in improving the effectiveness of these efforts and determine whether any of these databases should be added to the list of databases identified by CMS for screening purposes.
2. Collaborate with SSA to facilitate sharing CMS's DMF subscription with state Medicaid programs.
3. Coordinate with other federal agencies, as necessary, to explore the use of an identifier that is relevant for the screening of MMC plan providers and common across databases used to screen MMC plan providers.
4. Provide state Medicaid programs with guidance that establishes expectations and best practices on sharing provider screening data among states and MMC plans.

AGENCY AND THIRD-PARTY COMMENTS AND OUR EVALUATION

We provided a draft copy of this report to HHS. In its written comments, HHS described the actions it will take to address our first three recommendations. In response to our fourth recommendation to provide state Medicaid programs with guidance that establishes expectations and best practices on sharing provider screening data among states and Medicaid managed care plans, HHS commented that it developed the Medicaid provider termination notification database to assist states with the requirement to deny or terminate the enrollment of any provider that has been terminated for cause under Medicare or another state's Medicaid program or CHIP. It added that its Medicaid managed care proposed rule, issued in June 2015, if finalized, will require that state Medicaid programs enroll providers participating in Medicaid managed care. HHS stated that this will help ensure that all Medicaid managed care providers are screened against the Medicaid provider termination notification database. However, states' use of the Medicaid provider termination notification database is not required, not all states are using it, plans do not have access to the database, and the proposed rule does not address use of the database. Therefore, HHS's reported actions will not address these specific issues. HHS also provided technical comments, which we incorporated as appropriate.

We also provided relevant draft portions of this report to SSA, state Medicaid program offices for California, Florida, Illinois, Minnesota, Missouri, New Jersey, New York, Tennessee, Texas, and Washington, and representatives of the MMC plans. SSA provided technical comments which we incorporated as appropriate. States and plans were also in agreement with the draft portions they received, and provided some technical comments, which we incorporated as appropriate.

Sincerely yours,

Carolyn L. Yocom
Director, Health Care

Appendix I: Descriptions of Federal Databases Selected States and Medicaid Managed Care Plans Use to Screen Providers

Database	Description
Administrative Actions Against Registrants	The Drug Enforcement Administration (DEA) administers a provision of the Controlled Substances Act of 1970 that, among other things, requires all health care providers entitled to dispense, administer, or prescribe controlled pharmaceuticals; and all pharmacies entitled to fill prescriptions to register with the DEA. The Controlled Substances Act authorizes the DEA to take enforcement actions, such as administrative actions, against the registrant, for various reasons, such as materially falsifying the registration application filed; having been convicted of a felony relating to a controlled substance; having had its state license or registration suspended, revoked, or denied; or having been excluded from participation in a Medicaid or Medicare program. DEA's Administrative Actions Against Registrants shows, by year, DEA's administrative actions.

Appendix I. (Continued)

Database	Description
DEA Number	DEA Number is DEA's complete official database of persons and organizations certified to handle controlled substances under the Controlled Substances Act. DEA authorizes the use of this database, and the inclusion of any individual or organization in the database, as proof of that entity's registration with the DEA.
Designated Foreign Terrorist Organizations	The Department of State compiles a list of foreign organizations that are designated by the Secretary of State as Foreign Terrorist Organizations, in accordance with section 219 of the Immigration and Nationality Act, as amended.
Death Master File (DMF)	The Social Security Administration (SSA) compiles death information about Social Security number-holders in order to ensure it does not pay Social Security benefits to deceased individuals and to establish benefits for survivors. This information is in the agency's DMF. SSA obtains death reports from a variety of sources, including family members, funeral directors, post offices, financial institutions, other federal agencies, and states. To get death reports from the states, SSA has established formal agreements that set forth a payment structure for the states' death reports and limit SSA's ability to share this information. However, the Social Security Act requires SSA to share death information, to the extent feasible, including data reports by the states, with federal agencies to ensure proper payment of benefits to individuals. The act also prohibits SSA from sharing state-reported death information for any other purposes. As a result, SSA maintains two versions of the DMF. The full DMF, which contains all death records, is available to federal benefit payment agencies. The partial DMF, which excludes state-reported death information, is available publicly.
Denied Persons List	The list identifies individuals and entities that have been denied export privileges, by written order to the Department of Commerce.
Entity List	The Export Administration Regulations (EAR) contain licensing requirements for the export, re-export and/or transfer (in-country) of specified items. The Entity List contains names of certain foreign persons—including businesses, research institutions, government and private organizations, individuals, and other types of legal persons—that are subject to the EAR. On an individual basis, the persons on the Entity List are subject to licensing requirements and policies supplemental to those found in the EAR. The list is found on the Department of Commerce's Bureau of Industry and Security website.

Database	Description
Excluded Parties List System (EPLS)/ System of Award Management (SAM)	The General Services Administration (GSA) maintains the EPLS, an online system that includes information regarding parties debarred, suspended, proposed for debarment, excluded, or otherwise disqualified from receiving federal funds; in 2012, GSA migrated the EPLS into SAM. All federal agencies are required to send information to the EPLS on parties they have debarred or suspended. The EPLS provides only the name and address of excluded entities, but no other unique identifiers. The HHS-OIG also sends GSA monthly updates of the LEIE for inclusion in the EPLS, but the LEIE information included in EPLS does not provide all of the information from LEIE. For example, EPLS does not provide more details on LEIE excluded providers, such as the statutory basis for the exclusion action, date of birth, and address.
Federal Employees Health Benefits Program (FEHBP) Administrative Sanctions	The FEHBP provides coverage to federal employees, retirees, and their dependents through health insurance carriers that contract with the federal government. The Office of Personnel Management (OPM) negotiates these contracts and requires that each of these carriers establish a program to prevent, detect, and eliminate fraud and abuse. OPM's Office of Inspector General suspends and debars health care providers from the FEHBP who have, among other things, lost professional licenses, been convicted of a crime related to the delivery of or payment for health care services, violated provisions of a federal program, or been debarred by another federal agency. The names of such providers are available through the secure OPM Debar Webpage. The list of sanctioned providers is also available to the public through SAM—GSA's government-wide list of exclusions.
List of Excluded Individuals and Entities (LEIE)	The Department of Health and Human Services Office of Inspector General (HHS-OIG) maintains and updates monthly the LEIE, a database of providers it has excluded. The LEIE includes information on excluded providers, such as providers' names, addresses, dates of birth, occupation at the time of exclusion, provider type, and the statutory basis for the exclusion. The LEIE is publicly available to search or download on the HHS-OIG website, and available in two formats: online and downloadable. The online search engine identifies currently excluded individuals and entities. When a match is identified, it is possible to verify the accuracy of the match using a Social Security number or employer identification number. The downloadable version of the database may be compared against state enrollment files. However, unlike the online version, the downloadable version does not include Social Security number or employer identification number.

Appendix I. (Continued)

Database	Description
Look Up a Zip Code	A United States Postal Service website that allows zip code searches by address, city, and state.
Medicare Exclusion Database (MED)	CMS developed the MED in 2002 to collect and retrieve information that aided in ensuring that no payments are made to excluded individuals and entities for services furnished during the exclusion period. According to CMS, MED files contain a variety of identifiable and general information including names, Social Security numbers, National Provider Identifiers, addresses, exclusion types, and reinstatement dates, if applicable. CMS uses the HHS-OIG's LEIE to populate the MED; the HHS-OIG sends monthly updates of the LEIE to CMS.
Medicare Opt-out List	The Medicare Opt-out List is a list of physicians and practitioners who do not wish to enroll in the Medicare program and have "opted-out" of Medicare. This means that neither the provider, nor the beneficiary submits the bill to Medicare for services rendered. Instead, the beneficiary pays the provider out-of-pocket and neither party is reimbursed by Medicare.
National Plan and Provider Enumeration System (NPPES)	The National Provider Identifier (NPI) is a national, unique 10-digit identification number assigned to health care providers that CMS adopted to be used in specified administrative and financial transactions for its health care providers and suppliers in accordance with the Health Insurance Portability and Accountability Act. CMS uses NPPES to assign NPIs to providers.
National Practitioner Data Bank (NPDB)	NPDB, maintained by the Health Resources and Services Administration, an agency within HHS, is an information clearinghouse containing information related to the professional competence and conduct of healthcare providers. The NPDB is intended to facilitate a comprehensive review of professional credentials of health care providers and collects information on adverse licensing and certification actions, criminal convictions (health care related), civil judgments, exclusions from federal or state health care programs, and other adjudicated actions or decisions, medical malpractice payments, and any negative actions or findings taken by peer review organizations. It includes LEIE exclusions and related reinstatement actions taken by the HHS-OIG. However, because the criteria for inclusion in the NPDB are different than the criteria for inclusion in the LEIE, not all LEIE exclusions are listed in the NPDB.
OIG Most Wanted Fugitives	This HHS-OIG webpage includes the names of its most wanted fugitives on charges related to health care fraud and abuse.

Database	Description
Politically Exposed Persons	This is the Federal Financial Institutions Examination Council's list of current, senior foreign political figures, their immediate family, and their close associates, who potentially pose a risk that their funds may be the proceeds of foreign corruption.
Provider Enrollment, Chain and Ownership System (PECOS)	PECOS is an Internet-based system to which Medicare providers submit and update their enrollment data. In response to the Patient Protection and Affordable Care Act's requirement for CMS to establish a process for sharing information about terminated Medicare providers with state agencies, CMS provided states direct access to PECOS, where they can view specific enrollment data for each provider including identifying information such as National Provider Identifiers, tax identification numbers (TINs), and legal business names. PECOS also includes information on revoked licenses and terminated Medicare providers. While the data stored in the system are specific to Medicare providers, they are useful to state Medicaid programs. For example, states may use the data when screening providers during enrollment processes to determine whether a provider has ever been excluded from participation in Medicare and, thus, whether they should be allowed to participate in Medicaid. They also use PECOS data during provider screening to determine whether a Medicare screening has already taken place, thus eliminating the need to screen further for Medicaid participation.
Public Access to Court Electronic Records (PACER)	PACER is an electronic public access service that allows users to obtain case and docket information online from federal appellate, district, and bankruptcy courts, and the PACER Case Locator. PACER is provided by the federal judiciary in keeping with its commitment to providing public access to court information via a centralized service.
Specially Designated Nationals List	As part of its enforcement efforts, the Office of Foreign Assets Control, within the Department of Treasury, publishes a list of individuals and companies owned or controlled by, or acting for or on behalf of, targeted countries. It also lists individuals, groups, and entities—such as terrorists and narcotics traffickers—designated under programs that are not country-specific. Collectively, such individuals are blocked and U.S. persons are generally prohibited from dealing with them.
Taxpayer Identification Number Matching	The Internal Revenue Service's TIN Matching is part of a suite of Internet based pre-filing e-services that allows "authorized payers" the opportunity to match 1099 payee information against Internal Revenue Service records prior to filing information returns.

Appendix I. (Continued)

Database	Description
	An authorized payer is one who has filed forms 1099-B, 1099-DIV, 1099-INT, 1099-K, 1099-MISC, 1099-OID, or 1099-PATR with the Internal Revenue Service in at least one of the two past tax years. Interactive TIN Matching will accept up to 25 payee TIN/name combinations on-screen, while Bulk TIN Matching will allow up to 100,000 payee TIN/name combinations to be matched via a text file submission. Both programs will match the payee name and TIN with Internal Revenue Service records; decrease backup withholding and penalty notices; and reduce the error rate in TIN validation.
Unverified List	Parties listed on the Department of Commerce's Unverified List are ineligible to receive items subject to the Export Administration Regulations by means of a license exception. In addition, exporters must file an Automated Export System record for all exports to parties listed on the Unverified List and obtain a statement from such parties prior to exporting, re-exporting, or transferring to such parties any item subject to the Export Administration Regulations that is not subject to a license requirement.
Wanted Fugitives	This is the Federal Bureau of Investigation's list of wanted fugitives.

Source: GAO review of documentation on various federal databases identified by selected states and Medicaid managed care plans. | GAO-16-402.

End Notes

[1] Office of the Actuary, Centers for Medicare & Medicaid Services, United States Department of Health and Human Services: 2014 Actuarial Report on the Financial Outlook for Medicaid, (Washington, D.C.: 2014).

[2] See GAO, High-Risk Series: An Update, GAO-15-290 (Washington, D.C.: Feb. 11, 2015).

[3] An improper payment is any payment that should not have been made or that was made in an incorrect amount (including overpayments and underpayments) under statutory, contractual, administrative, or other legally applicable requirements. It includes any payment to an ineligible recipient, any payment for an ineligible service, any duplicate payment, payment for services not received (except where authorized by law), and any payment that does not account for credit for applicable discounts. Improper Payments Elimination and Recovery Act of 2010, Pub. L. No. 111-204, § 2(e), 124 Stat. 2224, 2227 (codified at 31 U.S.C. § 3321 note).

[4] See GAO, Medicaid: HCFA and States Could Work Together to Better Ensure the Integrity of Providers, GAO/T-HEHS-00-159 (Washington, D.C.: July 18, 2000).

[5] See GAO, Medicaid: Additional Actions Needed to Help Improve Provider and Beneficiary Fraud Controls, GAO-15-313 (Washington, D.C.: May 14, 2015).

[6] See GAO, Medicaid Program Integrity: State and Federal Efforts to Prevent and Detect Improper Payments, GAO-04-707 (Washington, D.C.: July 16, 2004); and GAO/T-HEHS-00-159.

[7] States may have different types of managed care arrangements in Medicaid. In this report, where we refer to Medicaid managed care, we are generally referring to comprehensive, risk-based managed care, the most common type of managed care arrangement.

[8] Pub. L. No. 111-148, 124 Stat.119 (2010), as amended by the Health Care and Education Reconciliation Act of 2010 (HCERA), Pub. L. No. 111-152, 124 Stat. 1029 (2010), which we refer to collectively as PPACA. PPACA permitted states to expand their Medicaid programs by covering certain low-income adults not historically eligible for Medicaid coverage; as of May 2015, 29 states elected to do so. States that choose to expand their Medicaid programs under PPACA have generally done so with managed care arrangements.

[9] See GAO, A Framework for Managing Fraud Risks in Federal Programs, GAO-15-593SP (Washington, D.C.: July 28, 2015). Also see, GAO, Standards for Internal Control in the Federal Government, GAO-14-704G (Washington, D.C.: Sept. 10, 2014). Internal control is a process affected by an entity's oversight body, management, and other personnel that provides reasonable assurance that the objectives of an entity will be achieved.

[10] See 42 C.F.R. § 455.410 (2015).

[11] In June 2015, CMS issued a proposed rule that would, if finalized, require all MMC plan providers to enroll with the state Medicaid agency and, as a result, subject all MMC plan providers to the same screening requirements as Medicaid FFS providers. See Medicaid Managed Care, CHIP Delivered in Managed Care, Medicaid and CHIP Comprehensive Quality Strategies, and Revisions to Third Party Liability, 80 Fed. Reg. 31098 (proposed June 1, 2015).

In addition, Congress is considering legislation, The Ensuring Removal of Terminated Providers from Medicaid and CHIP Act, which would require all providers participating in Medicaid to enroll with the state, regardless of whether the provider services Medicaid beneficiaries on a FFS basis or through a managed care entity. See H.R. 3716, 114th Cong. (2nd Sess. 2016).

[12] See GAO-15-313.

[13] In this report, we focus on individuals and entities providing Medicaid services. We do not cover directors, officers, partners, and other persons with ownership and control in an MMC plan.

[14] See 42 U.S.C. § 1396b(i)(2).

[15] See 42 U.S.C. § 1396a(a)(39), 42 C.F.R. § 455.416(c) (2015).

[16] See 42 C.F.R. § 455.101 (2015).

[17] See 42 C.F.R. § 455.101 (2015). In the preamble to its final rule, CMS stated that for cause does not include cases where a state terminates an inactive provider from its enrollment files, or where a provider takes voluntary action to end its participation in the program, except where that voluntary action is taken to avoid sanction. See Medicare, Medicaid, and Children's Health Insurance Programs; Additional Screening Requirements, Application Fees, Temporary Enrollment Moratoria, Payment Suspensions and Compliance Plans for Providers and Suppliers, 76 Fed. Reg. 5862, 5943 (Feb. 2, 2011).

[18] See 42 U.S.C. § 1395cc(j)(2); 42 C.F.R. § 455.410 (2015). As previously noted, these regulations would also apply to any states that elected to enroll MMC plan providers. Two of the states in our review enrolled MMC plan providers and were subject to these minimum requirements, although they had flexibility to establish more stringent requirements. 42 C.F.R § 455.452 (2015).

[19] 42 C.F.R. § 455.436(b) (2015) requires states to check the Excluded Parties List System (EPLS). However, the General Services Administration discontinued EPLS in 2012 and moved its content to the System for Award Management (SAM). In August 2012, CMS officials instructed states to use SAM instead of EPLS to fulfill their regulatory responsibilities.

[20] See Toolkits for Frequent Findings: 42 CFR 455.436 (December 2014).

[21] See Centers for Medicare & Medicaid Services, The Medicaid Managed Care Plan's Role in Preventing, Detecting, and Reporting Fraud, Waste, and Abuse (October 2014); and Centers for Medicare & Medicaid Services, Managed Care Plans: Critical Partner in the Fight against Fraud Waste, and Abuse in Medicaid-Presentation (September 2014).

[22] These two states also enroll their MMC plan providers, which means that they are subject to the same regulatory requirements for database use that apply to the screening of FFS plan providers, i.e., states should check all four databases—Death Master File, National Provider Enumeration System, List of Excluded Individuals and Entities, and the Exluded Parties List System. Officials from the state that did not use the Death Master File at the time of our review told us that they were aware of this requirement and they were in the process of procuring a subscription for the Death Master File.

[23] See GAO-14-704G.

[24] Cost of the Death Master File was also identified as an impediment to access by participants in a forum sponsored by GAO. See GAO, Data Analytics for Oversight & Law Enforcement, GAO-13-680SP (Washington, D.C.: July 15, 2013).

[25] Participants in a 2013 forum sponsored by GAO also identified the lack of a common identifier across databases as a challenge to accurately identifying individuals and entities. See GAO-13-680SP.

[26] See GAO-14-704G, 13.01–13.06.

[27] See GAO-15-313.

[28] Federal Improper Payments Coordination Act of 2015, Pub. L. No. 114-109, § 2, 129 Stat. 2225 (2015).

[29] CMS established the Medicaid provider termination notification system, commonly referred to as TIBCO, an online portal, in response to a PPACA requirement to establish a process to make available to state agencies information about providers terminated for cause from the Medicare, Medicaid, and CHIP programs, which could help to prevent a provider who has been terminated for cause in one state from enrolling in another state. According to CMS officials, states can upload information on providers they have terminated and download data on providers other states have terminated; however, neither action is required. According to the officials, the Medicaid provider termination notification system is the most centralized source of data available on state ineligible providers. The HHS-OIG raised this issue in a 2014 report and recommended that CMS require each state to submit terminated provider reports. See Department of Health and Human Services, Office of Inspector General, CMS's Process for Sharing Information About Terminated Providers Needs Improvement, March 2014 (OEI-06-12-00031).

[30] Congress is considering legislation that would require that states report to the Secretary of Health and Human Services identifying information about a provider terminated for cause or other reasons specified by the Secretary from participating in the state's Medicaid program. The bill also proposed that the Secretary of HHS include providers terminated from participation in Medicare, Medicaid, or CHIP in a termination database or similar system, within 21 days of notification of the termination. See H.R. 3716, 114th Cong. (2nd Sess. 2016).

[31] According to a vendor that performs MMC plan screenings, only 37 states and the District of Columbia made their data on ineligible providers publicly available, as of November 2015. CMS officials said they do not track this information. However, various third party vendors specialize in the collection of ineligible provider information. States and MMC plans can contract with these vendors to monitor provider eligibility status continuously.

[32] The HHS-OIG also raised this issue in a 2015 report that found that inconsistent terminology on exclusions among the states and HHS-OIG made it difficult for states to distinguish between providers who were eligible to participate in Medicaid and those that were excluded. See Department of Health and Human Services, Office of Inspector General, Providers Terminated from One State Medicaid program Continued to Participating in Other States, August 2015 (OEI-06-12-00030).

[33] 42 C.F.R. § 1002.212 (2015) requires that when a state agency initiates an exclusion, it must notify other state agencies, the state medical licensing board (where applicable), the public, and beneficiaries.

[34] See GAO-14-04G.

In: Medicaid Managed Care
Editor: Geneva Barrett

ISBN: 978-1-63485-817-5

Chapter 3

MEDICAID: SERVICE UTILIZATION PATTERNS FOR BENEFICIARIES IN MANAGED CARE*

United States Government Accountability Office

WHY GAO DID THIS STUDY

Medicaid, a federal-state health financing program for low-income and medically needy individuals, covered 65 million beneficiaries at an estimated cost of $508 billion in fiscal year 2014. More than half of Medicaid beneficiaries are enrolled in managed care plans, a health care delivery model where states contract with managed care organizations to provide covered services for a set cost. Historically, states have submitted relatively unreliable managed care service utilization data, also known as encounter data, to the Centers for Medicare & Medicaid Services, the federal agency that oversees Medicaid. However, recent evidence suggests that encounter data may be improving. Information on beneficiaries' service utilization could serve as a baseline for future analyses of utilization trends over time. GAO was asked to examine the level of services provided to these beneficiaries. In this report, GAO describes what encounter data indicate about the service utilization of Medicaid beneficiaries in managed care plans.

* This is an edited, reformatted and augmented version of the United States Government Accountability Office publication, GAO-15-481, dated May 2015.

To do this work, GAO analyzed state- reported data included in CMS's 2010 Medicaid Analytic eXtract data and determined that 19 states had data that were reliable for its purposes, but excluded the remaining 31 states and the District of Columbia. For these 19 states, GAO calculated service utilization rates for adult and child beneficiaries enrolled in comprehensive managed care plans by state, service category, and length of enrollment. GAO received technical comments on a draft of this report from HHS and incorporated them as appropriate.

WHAT GAO FOUND

Based on GAO's analysis of 2010 encounter data reported by 19 states, the number of professional services utilized by adult beneficiaries ranged from about 13 to 55. For children, the number of professional services utilized per beneficiary was lower, ranging from about 6 to 16 among the 19 states. Professional services included four categories of services: (1) evaluation and management (E/M) services, such as office visits and emergency room and critical care services; (2) procedural services, such as surgery and ophthalmology; (3) ancillary services, such as pathology and lab services; and (4) other professional services, such as oxygen therapy.

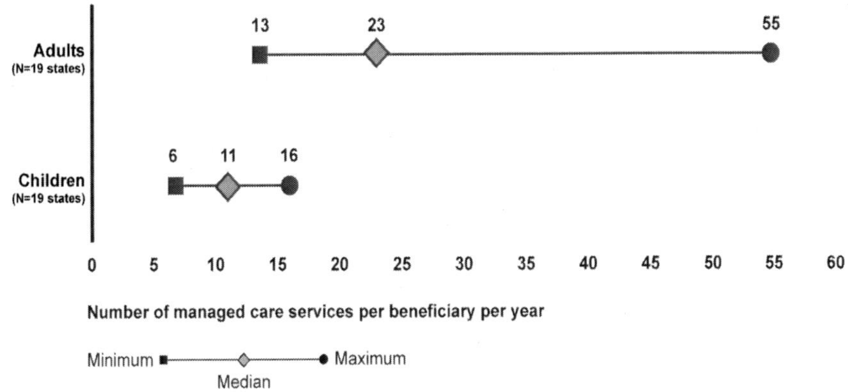

Source: GAO analysis of Medicaid Analytic eXtract data. | GAO-15-481

Adult and Child Professional Service Utilization in Selected States, 2010.

States varied considerably in how service utilization was distributed within service categories. For example, of total services,

- adult per beneficiary utilization of ancillary services ranged from 37 percent in Rhode Island to 65 percent in Washington and Illinois; and
- child per beneficiary utilization of E/M services ranged from 29 percent in Minnesota to 45 percent in Georgia and Rhode Island.

Service utilization for both adult and child beneficiaries also varied by the length of enrollment. When compared with beneficiaries enrolled for a full year, total service utilization for adults was 2 to 78 percent higher for partial-year beneficiaries—those enrolled in a comprehensive managed care plan for less than the full year—in slightly more than half of selected states. For children in all but one selected state, service utilization was 4 to 44 percent higher for partial- year beneficiaries compared with full-year beneficiaries.

ABBREVIATIONS

CMS	Centers for Medicare & Medicaid Services
CHIP	State Children's Health Insurance Program
E/M	evaluation and management
FFS	fee-for-service
HCPCS	Healthcare Common Procedural Coding System
MCO	managed care organization
MAX	Medicaid Analytic eXtract
MSIS	Medicaid Statistical Information System
PPACA	Patient Protection and Affordable Care Act

***

May 29, 2015

The Honorable Ron Wyden
Ranking Member
Committee on Finance
United States Senate

Dear Senator Wyden:

Medicaid, a federal-state health financing program for low-income and medically needy individuals, served approximately 65 million beneficiaries at a total cost of about $508 billion in fiscal year 2014. More than half of those beneficiaries are enrolled in managed care plans. As Medicaid spending and enrollment grew in recent years, states increasingly turned to the managed care delivery model as a way to provide services to Medicaid beneficiaries. Under this delivery model, states typically contract with managed care organizations (MCO) to provide a specific set of Medicaid-covered services to beneficiaries. The state pays the MCOs a set amount per beneficiary per month to provide the specific services covered under each managed care plan.[1]

The state expansions of Medicaid under the Patient Protection and Affordable Care Act (PPACA) increased the size of the Medicaid program, as well as the number of beneficiaries enrolled in managed care plans.[2] Since 1999, states have submitted data on managed care service utilization, also known as encounter data, to the Centers for Medicare & Medicaid Services (CMS), the federal agency that oversees Medicaid. Historically, these encounter data have been relatively incomplete and unreliable; thus, little is known about the utilization of services by Medicaid beneficiaries enrolled in managed care plans. However, recent evidence suggests that the quality of Medicaid encounter data may be improving and stronger requirements surrounding encounter data submissions suggest that such improvements could continue.[3] Analyses of beneficiaries' service utilization could enhance program knowledge and serve as a baseline for future analyses of trends in utilization over time and of the factors that may contribute to differences across states. You asked us to examine the level of services provided to beneficiaries in Medicaid managed care. In this report, we describe what encounter data indicate about the service utilization of Medicaid beneficiaries enrolled in managed care plans.

To describe what encounter data indicate about the service utilization of Medicaid beneficiaries enrolled in managed care plans, we analyzed Medicaid Analytic eXtract (MAX) data for calendar year 2010—the most recent data available at the time of our analysis.[4] To assess the reliability and usability of the MAX data for our purposes, we reviewed related documentation, such as studies that assessed the reliability of or analyzed MAX data, and we interviewed officials from CMS and its contractor responsible for processing the MAX data. We determined that 19 states reported data that were reliable for our purposes: Arizona, Connecticut, Delaware, Florida, Georgia, Illinois,

Indiana, Kentucky, Michigan, Minnesota, Nebraska, New Mexico, New York, Oregon, Rhode Island, Tennessee, Texas, Virginia, and Washington.[5] However, we excluded the other 31 states and the District of Columbia because we determined their data were unreliable or otherwise were not usable for our purposes.[6]

For the 19 selected states, we identified adult and child beneficiaries who were enrolled in a comprehensive managed care plan in at least one month during calendar year 2010, and identified four broad categories of professional services: (1) evaluation and management (E/M) services; (2) procedural services; (3) ancillary services; and (4) other professional services.[7] To determine utilization rates for identified services, we calculated the number of services used per adult and child beneficiary per year by state, service category, and length of enrollment.[8] The results we present are based on data reported to CMS by the 19 states in our analysis, and are not representative of all states and their managed care programs. Our results also do not offer conclusions regarding whether the level of service utilization identified is appropriate.[9] Finally, there are a number of state-specific factors—such as differences in beneficiary health status and provider supply—that could contribute to variation in service utilization across the states, and attributing this variation to specific factors was beyond the scope of this study. (See appendix I for a detailed description of our methodology and study limitations.)

We conducted this performance audit from November 2013 to May 2015 in accordance with generally accepted government auditing standards. Those standards require that we plan and perform the audit to obtain sufficient, appropriate evidence to provide a reasonable basis for our findings and conclusions based on our audit objectives. We believe that the evidence obtained provides a reasonable basis for our findings and conclusions based on our audit objectives.

BACKGROUND

Delivery Models for Medicaid Services

Managed care and fee-for-service (FFS) are two possible models that states use to deliver benefits under their Medicaid programs. Most states provide a combination of these two delivery models, which offer different financial incentives.

Nationally, more than half of Medicaid beneficiaries are enrolled in a managed care plan. States contract with MCOs to provide a specific set of Medicaid-covered services to beneficiaries, and MCOs are expected to report encounter data to state Medicaid programs that allow the Medicaid administrators to track the services received by enrolled beneficiaries. The state pays the MCO a predetermined amount per beneficiary per month—known as capitation—and, in turn, the MCO pays providers for their services. According to CMS, by contracting with various types of Medicaid MCOs to deliver services, states can reduce program costs and better manage utilization of health care services. However, since MCOs receive a fixed amount per beneficiary regardless of the number of services used, we have noted in our prior work that there may be financial incentives for MCOs to limit access to services, potentially compromising quality of care and leading to underutilization of services.[10]

Historically, most Medicaid programs relied on a FFS delivery model. Under the FFS model, states pay providers directly for each service provided to a Medicaid beneficiary and the data included on a Medicaid FFS claim includes a specific amount for services delivered to a beneficiary. Certain states continue to use the FFS model to provide Medicaid services, such as behavioral health and dental care. We have noted in our prior work that, unlike managed care, the FFS model may give providers an incentive to use more services than necessary.[11]

Efforts to Analyze Utilization Using Medicaid Encounter Data

Despite the fact that states have been required to submit encounter data to CMS since 1999,[12] little is known about the utilization of services by Medicaid beneficiaries in MCOs. Historically, encounter data have been relatively incomplete and unreliable; thus, little is known about these data. At the behest of CMS, Mathematica Policy Research published a number of studies focused primarily on the usability and completeness of 2007-2010 Medicaid encounter data, as reported in MAX. These studies first reported that encounter data were suitable for research purposes in 2012.[13]

CMS has provided guidance to states on methods to improve the completeness and accuracy of encounter data.[14] In 2012, CMS released a protocol for validating Medicaid encounter data that states receive from MCOs. The protocol specifies a procedure for assessing the completeness and accuracy of encounter data that Medicaid MCOs are required to submit.

Additionally, PPACA strengthened the requirement that Medicaid MCOs provide encounter data to states by withholding federal matching payments from states that do not report encounter data to CMS in a timely manner.[15]

Factors Affecting Medicaid Managed Care Service Utilization

The service utilization patterns of beneficiaries enrolled in Medicaid managed care plans can vary substantially and be related to a variety of factors, including the characteristics of beneficiaries and the scope of state Medicaid benefits offered.[16]

- **Beneficiary participation in managed care**: States vary in the populations enrolled in managed care plans. States that enroll their most medically needy beneficiaries into managed care plans are likely to have higher service utilization. Conversely, states that enroll broader, generally healthier populations—such as children—into managed care plans are likely to have a larger pool of beneficiaries and potentially lower service utilization.
- **The amount, duration, and scope of services covered by MCOs**: Consistent with federal requirements, a state may determine the amount, duration, and the scope of benefits covered in their Medicaid programs.[17] Thus, variations in service utilization patterns could reflect states' benefit choices that are independent of their service delivery choices.
- **Variation in Medicaid managed care payments**: Medicaid MCO payments to providers for specific services vary substantially across states and this variation could affect the service utilization of beneficiaries. Specifically, we previously reported that in 23 states where we compared MCO and private insurance payments for E/M services, managed care payments were 31 to 65 percent lower in 18 states.[18]
- **Access to Providers**: Access to providers who serve beneficiaries enrolled in Medicaid managed care plans can vary substantially within a state, such as between urban and rural areas, and also across states.[19] Geographic variation in provider access, which can be driven by the breadth of an MCO's network and the availability of providers in a given geographic area, can affect the type and amount of services used by beneficiaries.

Beneficiaries' Service Utilization Varied by State, Population, Service Categories, and Length of Enrollment for Selected States

Based on our analysis of encounter data, the number of professional services utilized by adult and child beneficiaries per year in the 19 selected states ranged widely, with adult beneficiaries typically receiving more services. States also varied in how adult and child service utilization for professional services were distributed across service categories, and by whether beneficiaries were enrolled in comprehensive managed care plans for all of 2010 or part of the year.

A detailed, interactive display of the data used to support our findings is available at http://www.gao.gov/products/GAO-15-481.

Adult Service Utilization Ranged from 13 to 55 Services per Beneficiary per Year in Selected States

For the 19 selected states, the number of services per beneficiary per year for adults ranged from about 13 to 55 services per beneficiary per year.[20] (See figure 1.) Services used by adult beneficiaries included E/M services, such as office visits and emergency room and critical care services; procedural services, such as surgery and ophthalmology; ancillary services, such as pathology and lab services and anesthesiology; and other professional services, such as oxygen therapy and hospital-mandated on-call service. Service utilization levels for adult beneficiaries are affected by many factors, including the extent to which they receive services on a FFS basis. Among the states in our analysis, the percentage of professional services that adult beneficiaries received on a FFS basis ranged from 0 to about 11 percent, with a median of 1 percent.[21]

Service utilization among adults was concentrated primarily in the ancillary and E/M categories. Specifically, ancillary services were the largest category in all but one state and accounted for 53 percent, on average, of all services utilized by adult beneficiaries across selected states. E/M services made up the second largest category (27 percent), followed by procedural services (15 percent) and, lastly, other professional services (4 percent). However, states varied considerably in how service utilization was distributed within service categories, as was shown in figure 1.

- **Ancillary**: Of total services, adult per beneficiary utilization of ancillary services ranged from 37 percent in Rhode Island to 65 percent in Washington and Illinois—a difference of about 28 percentage points. Pathology/lab services accounted for 63 percent, on average, of all ancillary service utilization across selected states.
- **E/M**: Of total services, adult per beneficiary utilization of E/M services ranged from 19 percent in Connecticut to 38 percent in Rhode Island—a difference of 19 percentage points. Office visits accounted for 68 percent on average, of E/M service utilization, while emergency room and critical care services accounted for 16 percent, on average.
- **Procedural**: Of total services, adult per beneficiary utilization of procedural services ranged from 8 percent in Illinois to 23 percent in Indiana—a difference of about 15 percentage points. Surgical services accounted for the largest portion—36 percent, on average— of all procedural service utilization across selected states.
- **Other professional services**: Of total services, adult per beneficiary utilization of other professional services ranged from 1 percent in Illinois, Kentucky, Nebraska, and Washington to 15 percent in Arizona—a difference of about 15 percentage points.

For slightly more than half of the selected states, total service utilization among adults was higher for partial-year beneficiaries—those in comprehensive managed care plans for less than the full-year of 2010.[22] Specifically, in 11 of the 19 states, the number of services utilized per year ranged from 2 to 78 percent higher for partial-year beneficiaries than for full-year beneficiaries. In the remaining 8 states, service utilization for partial-year beneficiaries was 3 to 15 percent lower than for full-year beneficiaries. Of the states that had comparatively higher service utilization for partial-year beneficiaries, there were generally no major differences in service utilization among partial-year beneficiaries based on the length of their enrollment. Specifically, partial-year beneficiaries who were enrolled for 1 to 3 months, 4 to 6 months, or 7 to 11 months generally had similarly high utilization rates.

Further, we found that partial-year adult beneficiaries utilized more procedural and ancillary services than full-year beneficiaries in about two-thirds of the selected states. Among those states, partial-year adult beneficiaries used 19 and 26 percent more of these services, respectively, than full-year adult beneficiaries. (See figure 2.)

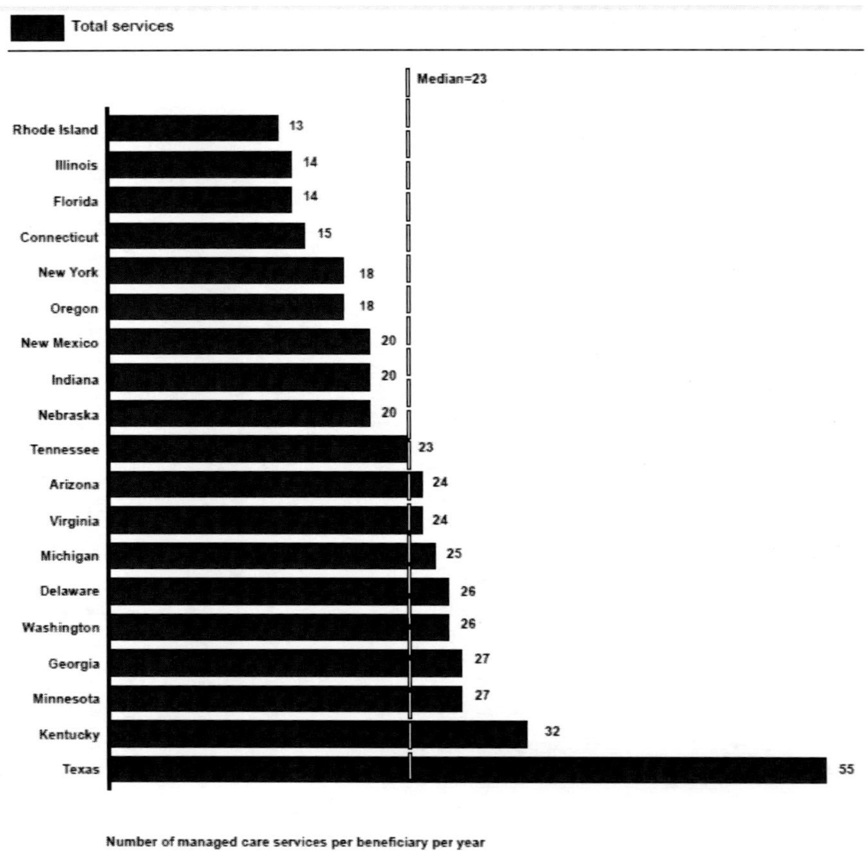

Total services
Median=23
Rhode Island
13
Illinois
14
Florida
14
Connecticut
15
New York
18
Oregon
18
New Mexico
20
Indiana
20
Nebraska
20
Tennessee
23
Arizona
24
Virginia
24
Michigan
25
Delaware
26
Washington
26
Georgia
27
Minnesota
27
Kentucky
32
Texas
55
Number of managed care services per beneficiary per year

Source: GAO analysis of Medicaid Analytic eXtract for calendar year 2010. | GAO-15-481

Notes: Beneficiaries included in our analysis were eligible to receive full Medicaid benefits and were enrolled in a comprehensive managed care plan in at least one month during calendar year 2010. We excluded beneficiaries who were enrolled in a comprehensive managed care plan if during the calendar year of our analysis they had other sources of health coverage in addition to Medicaid. We focused our analysis on professional services and excluded dental and behavioral health services and any services paid on a fee-for-service basis. Evaluation and management (E/M) services include services such as office visits and emergency room and critical care services. Procedural services include services such as surgery and ophthalmology. Ancillary services include services such as pathology and lab services, and anesthesiology. Other professional services include services such as oxygen therapy, hospital-mandated on-call service, and other services that are not otherwise classified in the categories above. See appendix I for more information. For the percentage of partial-year beneficiaries by state, see appendix III. Numbers are rounded to the nearest whole number except for the other professional services category. The percentages of total services in each state attributable to specific service categories were calculated based on unrounded data. A detailed, interactive display of the data used to support our findings is available at http://www.gao.gov/products/GAO-15-481.

Figure 1. Adult Professional Service Utilization in Selected States, 2010. See Table 3 in Appendix II for additional information on Figure 1 categories.

Total services

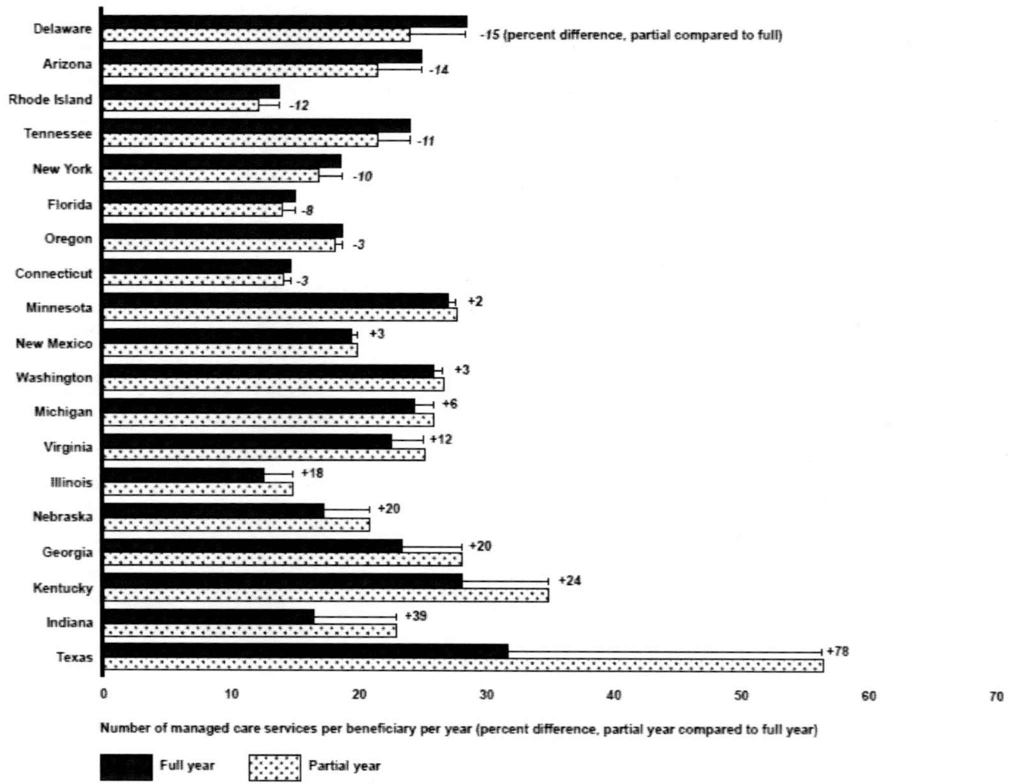

Source: GAO analysis of Medicaid Analytic eXtract for calendar year 2010. | GAO-15-481

Notes: Beneficiaries included in our analysis were eligible to receive full Medicaid benefits and were enrolled in a comprehensive managed care plan in at least one month during calendar year 2010. Partial-year beneficiaries are defined as those enrolled in a comprehensive managed care plan in calendar year 2010 for a period of less than 12 months. We weighted our results by the number of months each beneficiary was enrolled in comprehensive managed care in calendar year 2010 to account for beneficiaries who may have been enrolled for only part of the year. We excluded beneficiaries who were enrolled in a comprehensive managed care plan if during the calendar year of our analysis they had other sources of health coverage in addition to Medicaid. We focused our analysis on professional services and excluded dental and behavioral health services and any services paid on a fee-for-service basis. Evaluation and management (E/M) services include services such as office visits and emergency room and critical care services. Procedural services include services such as surgery and ophthalmology. Ancillary services include services such as pathology and lab services, and anesthesiology. Other professional services include services such as oxygen therapy, hospital-mandated on-call service, and other services that are not otherwise classified in the categories above. See appendix I for more information. For the percentage of partial-year beneficiaries by state, see appendix III. Numbers are rounded to the nearest tenth except for the other professional services category. The percent difference for each state was calculated based on unrounded data. A detailed, interactive display of the data used to support our findings is available at http://www.gao.gov/products/GAO-15-481.

Figure 2. Adult Professional Service Utilization in Selected States, Partial Year Beneficiaries Compared with Full Year Beneficiaries, 2010. See Table 4 in Appendix II for additional information on Figure 2 categories.

Child Service Utilization Ranged from 6 to 16 Services per Beneficiary per Year in Selected States, and was Significantly Higher for Partial-Year Beneficiaries

The utilization of professional services by children was generally lower than adults in selected states. In the 19 selected states, the number of services per beneficiary per year for children ranged from about 6 to 16.[23] (See figure 3.) Services used by child beneficiaries included E/M services, such as office visits and emergency room and critical care services; procedural services, such as surgery and ophthalmology; ancillary services, such as pathology and lab services and anesthesiology; and other professional services, such as oxygen therapy and hospital- mandated on-call service. Service utilization for child beneficiaries is affected by many factors, including the extent to which beneficiaries receive services on a FFS basis. Among selected states, the percentage of professional services that child beneficiaries received on a FFS basis ranged from 0 to about 29 percent, with a median of 9 percent.[24]

In contrast to adults, for which service utilization consisted mostly of ancillary services, utilization for children was distributed more evenly across service categories. For example, on average, E/M services were utilized most commonly by children (37 percent of services), followed by procedural services (33 percent), ancillary services (24 percent), and other professional services (5 percent). However, considerable state variation existed within service categories, as was shown in figure 3.

- **E/M**: Of total services, child per beneficiary utilization of E/M services ranged from 29 percent in Minnesota to 45 percent in Georgia and Rhode Island—a difference of 16 percentage points. On average, office visits (58 percent) and preventive visits (22 percent) comprised most E/M service utilization across selected states.
- **Procedural**: Of total services, child per beneficiary utilization of procedural services ranged from 25 percent in Arizona to 41 percent in Oregon and Texas—a difference of 16 percentage points. On average, immunizations and injections (60 percent) made up the majority of procedural service utilization across selected states.

- **Ancillary**: Of total services, child per beneficiary utilization of ancillary services ranged from 17 percent in Oregon to 36 percent in Illinois—a difference of 19 percentage points. On average, pathology and lab services (63 percent) made up the majority of ancillary service utilization across selected states.
- **Other professional services**: Of total services, child per beneficiary utilization of other professional services ranged from 1 percent in Georgia, Illinois, and New York to 21 percent in Arizona—a difference of 20 percentage points.

Total service utilization among children was higher for partial-year beneficiaries—those enrolled in comprehensive managed care for less than the full year of 2010—than full-year beneficiaries for almost every selected state.[25] For example, for all but one state, the number of services utilized per year was 4 to 44 percent higher for partial-year child beneficiaries than for full-year child beneficiaries. In the remaining state, the number of services utilized per year for partial-year child beneficiaries was 5 percent less than for full-year child beneficiaries.

Further, partial-year child beneficiaries utilized more E/M and procedural services than full-year child beneficiaries across all selected states; specifically, partial-year child beneficiaries utilized 19 percent more E/M services and 22 percent more procedural services than full-year child beneficiaries. (See figure 4.)

Among selected states with higher utilization for partial-year child beneficiaries, most experienced the highest utilization for child beneficiaries who were enrolled for 1 to 3 months as compared with 4 to 6 months or 7 to 11 months. When compared with full-year child beneficiaries, partial-year child beneficiaries enrolled for 1 to 3 months utilized, on average, significantly more E/M and procedural services (61 percent and 34 percent, respectively). Furthermore, the increased utilization among child beneficiaries enrolled for 1 to 3 months was particularly pronounced for certain E/M, procedural, and ancillary services. We found the following examples:

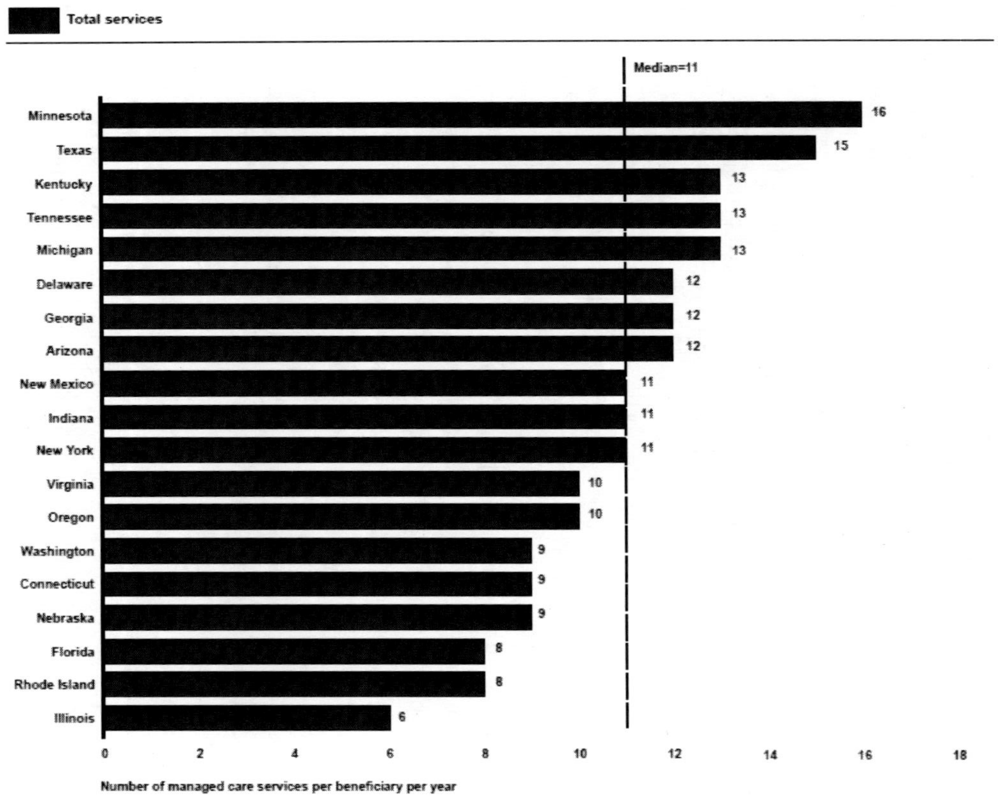

Source: GAO analysis of Medicaid Analytic eXtract for calendar year 2010. | GAO-15-481

Notes: Beneficiaries included in our analysis were eligible to receive full Medicaid benefits and were enrolled in a comprehensive managed care plan in at least one month during calendar year 2010. We excluded beneficiaries who were enrolled in a comprehensive managed care plan if during the calendar year of our analysis they had other sources of health coverage in addition to Medicaid. We focused our analysis on professional services and excluded dental and behavioral health services and any services paid on a fee-for-service basis. Evaluation and management (E/M) services include services such as office visits and emergency room and critical care services. Procedural services include services such as surgery and ophthalmology. Ancillary services include services such as pathology and lab services, and anesthesiology. Other professional services include services such as oxygen therapy, hospital-mandated on-call service, and other services that are not otherwise classified in the categories above. See appendix I for more information. For the percentage of partial-year beneficiaries by state, see appendix III. Numbers are rounded to the nearest whole number except for the other professional services category. The percentages of total services in each state attributable to specific service categories were calculated based on unrounded data. A detailed, interactive display of the data used to support our findings is available at http://www.gao.gov/products/GAO-15-481.

Figure 3. Child Professional Service Utilization in Selected States, 2010. See Table 5 in Appendix II for additional information on Figure 3 categories.

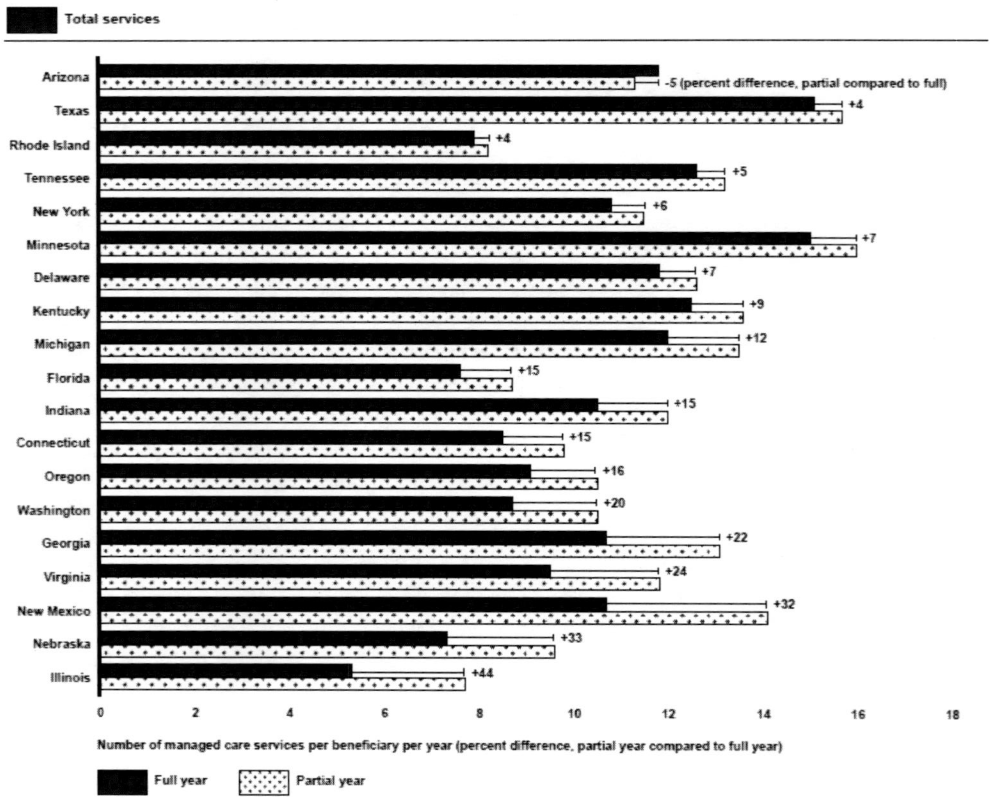

Source: GAO analysis of Medicaid Analytic eXtract for calendar year 2010. | GAO-15-481

Notes: Beneficiaries included in our analysis were eligible to receive full Medicaid benefits and were enrolled in a comprehensive managed care plan in at least one month during calendar year 2010. Partial-year beneficiaries are defined as those enrolled in a comprehensive managed care plan in calendar year 2010 for a period of less than 12 months. We weighted our results by the number of months each beneficiary was enrolled in comprehensive managed care in calendar year 2010 to account for beneficiaries who may have been enrolled for only part of the year. We excluded beneficiaries who were enrolled in a comprehensive managed care plan if during the calendar year of our analysis they had other sources of health coverage in addition to Medicaid. We focused our analysis on professional services and excluded dental and behavioral health services and any services paid on a fee-for-service basis. Evaluation and management (E/M) services include services such as office visits and emergency room and critical care services. Procedural services include services such as surgery and ophthalmology. Ancillary services include services such as pathology and lab services, and anesthesiology. Other professional services include services such as oxygen therapy, hospital-mandated on-call service, and other services that are not otherwise classified in the categories above. See appendix I for more information. For the percentage of partial-year beneficiaries by state, see appendix III. Numbers are rounded to the nearest tenth except for the other professional services category. The percent difference for each state was calculated based on unrounded data. A detailed, interactive display of the data used to support our findings is available at http://www.gao.gov/products/GAO-15-481.

Figure 4. Child Professional Service Utilization in Selected States, Partial Year Beneficiaries Compared with Full Year Beneficiaries, 2010. See Table 6 in Appendix II for additional information on Figure 4 categories.

- **Inpatient visits**: Across all selected states, utilization of inpatient visits ranged from 1.4 to over 15 times greater for child beneficiaries enrolled for 1 to 3 months than for full-year child beneficiaries.
- **Preventive services**: For all but one selected state, utilization of preventive visits ranged from 1.5 to almost 4 times greater for child beneficiaries enrolled for 1 to 3 months than for full-year child beneficiaries.
- **Emergency room and critical care**: For all but one selected state, utilization of emergency room and critical care services ranged from 1.2 to almost 3 times greater among child beneficiaries enrolled for 1 to 3 months than for full-year child beneficiaries.
- **Surgery**: For all but one selected state, utilization of surgery ranged from 1 to 2.5 times greater for child beneficiaries enrolled for 1 to 3 months than for full-year child beneficiaries.
- **Radiology**: Across all selected states, utilization of radiology ranged from 1.2 to 2.5 times greater for child beneficiaries enrolled for 1 to 3 months than for full-year child beneficiaries.

AGENCY COMMENTS

We provided the Secretary of Health and Human Services with a draft of this report. The Department of Health and Human Services provided technical comments, which we incorporated as appropriate.

Sincerely yours,

Carolyn L. Yocom
Director, Health Care

APPENDIX I: DETAILED SCOPE AND METHODOLOGY

We examined service utilization patterns for Medicaid beneficiaries enrolled in comprehensive managed care plans using Medicaid Analytic eXtract (MAX) encounter data for calendar year 2010,[26] the most recent year for which encounter data were available for the majority of states at the time we began our analyses.[27] Our analysis consisted of the following three steps:

(1) state selection, which included assessing data reliability for our selected states; (2) beneficiary and service identification; and (3) utilization calculation. Lastly, we present limitations of this study and technical comments that we received from 13 of the 19 selected states.

Step 1: State Selection

To assess the reliability and usability of the MAX data for our purposes, we reviewed related documentation and studies that assessed the reliability of or analyzed MAX data, and we interviewed officials from the Centers for Medicare & Medicaid Services (CMS) and its contractor responsible for processing the MAX data (Mathematica Policy Research, Inc.).[28] We determined that 19 states reported data that were reliable for our purposes: Arizona, Connecticut, Delaware, Florida, Georgia, Illinois, Indiana, Kentucky, Michigan, Minnesota, Nebraska, New Mexico, New York, Oregon, Rhode Island, Tennessee, Texas, Virginia, and Washington.[29]

We excluded the remaining 31 states and the District of Columbia because we determined their data were unreliable or not usable for our purposes for one or more of the following reasons: (1) no adults or children were enrolled in comprehensive managed care plans, according to MAX (13 states); (2) MAX data were unavailable at the time we began our analysis (11 states); (3) the data were unreliable, such as if fewer than 30 percent of beneficiaries used at least one service—one of the thresholds established by Mathematica when evaluating the completeness and usability of MAX data (6 states); and (4) services were not reported using a standard coding convention, namely the Health Care Common Procedural Coding System (HCPCS) (2 states).[30] (See table 1.)

Step 2: Beneficiary and Service Identification

Based on eligibility information in the MAX Person Summary file,[31] we restricted our study to adults and children who (1) were eligible to receive full Medicaid benefits and were enrolled for any given month during calendar year 2010, and (2) did not have other sources of health coverage during the calendar year in addition to Medicaid, such as coverage from Medicare or private insurance.[32] Our analysis accounted for 95 percent of the adults and children in comprehensive managed care among the 19 states in our analysis in 2010.

Table 1. States Included in Our Analysis and Reasons for State Exclusions

State	Included in analysis	Excluded from analysis	Reasons for Exclusion: No adults or children enrolled	Unavailable data	Unreliable data	Lacked standard coding
Alabama			√			
Alaska		√	√			
Arizona	√					
Arkansas		√	√			
California[c]		√			√	
Colorado[b]		√			√	
Connecticut	√					
Delaware	√					
District of Columbia[a,f]		√		√		
Florida	√					
Georgia	√					
Hawaii[d]		√				√
Idaho[a]		√		√		
Illinois	√					
Indiana	√					
Iowa		√	√			
Kansas[a]		√		√		
Kentucky	√					
Louisiana		√	√			
Maine[a]		√		√		
Maryland[d]		√				√
Massachusetts[a]		√		√		
Michigan	√					
Minnesota	√					
Mississippi		√	√			
Missouri[a]		√		√		
Montana[e]		√	√			
Nebraska	√					
Nevada[a]		√		√		
New Hampshire		√	√			

State	Included in analysis	Excluded from analysis	Reasons for Exclusion			
			No adults or children enrolled	Unavailable data	Unreliable data	Lacked standard coding
New Jersey[a]		√		√		
New Mexico	√					
New York	√					
North Carolina		√	√			
North Dakota[a]		√		√		
Ohio[b]		√			√	
Oklahoma		√	√			
Oregon	√					
Pennsylvania[b]		√			√	
Rhode Island	√					
South Carolina[b]		√			√	
South Dakota		√	√			
Tennessee	√					
Texas	√					
Utah[a]		√		√		
Vermont		√	√			
Virginia	√					
Washington	√					
West Virginia[b]		√			√	
Wisconsin[a]		√		√		
Wyoming		√	√			
Total	**19**	**32**	**13**	**11**	**6**	**2**

Source: GAO analysis of Centers for Medicare & Medicaid Services (CMS) and Medicaid Analytic eXtract data. | GAO-15-481

[a] State was not included in the November 2013 MAX data.

[b] We determined that data submitted by Colorado, Ohio, Pennsylvania, South Carolina, and West Virginia were unreliable because these states reported that fewer than 30 percent of beneficiaries enrolled in comprehensive managed care plans received managed care services.

[c] California was excluded from the analysis because both the state and CMS's contractor expressed specific concerns about the unreliability of the state's 2010 managed care data.

[d] Hawaii and Maryland did not report services using a five-digit Health Care Common Procedural Coding System code.

[e] While Montana had a small number of adults in comprehensive managed care plans, the state was excluded because its beneficiaries did not meet our beneficiary inclusion criteria of receiving full Medicaid benefits and not having other sources of health coverage.

[f] For the purpose of this table, the District of Columbia is counted as a state.

We used the MAX Other Services file to identify professional services used by beneficiaries while they were enrolled in a comprehensive managed care plan. We, in large part, used the Health Care Cost Institute's methodology for grouping professional services based on a range of HCPCS codes. These codes are used by providers to bill for professional services.[33] We grouped the professional services in our analysis into four broad categories. (See table 2.)

Table 2. Professional Service Categories and Related Procedure Codes Included in the Analysis

Professional Service Category	Subcategories	Related procedure codes
Evaluation and management	Consultations	99241–99255
	Emergency room/critical care	99281–99292, 99466–99476
	Inpatient visits	99217–99239, 99304–99340, 99477, 99478–99480
	Office visits	99201–99215, 99341–99350
	Preventive visits	99381–99387, 99391–99429, 99460–99464
	Other evaluation and management	90951-90970; 92605, 92607, 92608, 95251, 96004; 96150 - 96151; 98966-98969; 99024; 99354-99360; 99363-99380; 99441-99444; 99450-99456, 99499; 99605-99607
Procedural	Administered drugs, including chemo drugs	J0000–J9999
	Allergy	95004–95075, 95115–95199
	Cardiovascular	92950–93352, 93501–93581, 93600-93799, 93875–93990
	Immunizations/injections	90281–90749, 96360–96379, G0008–G0010
	Ophthalmology	92002–92499, V2020–V2799
	Surgery	10021–69990 excluding 36415–36416; 0016T–0222T

Professional Service Category	Subcategories	Related procedure codes
	Other procedural	90935 – 90947; 90989-90999; 91000-91299; 92502—92604, 92606; 92609-92633; 92640, 92700; 94002-94799; 95250; 95803-96003, 96020-96125; 96152-96155; 96401-96571; 96900-96999; 98960-98962; 99143-99199; 99465
Ancillary	Anesthesia	00100–02020, 99100–99140
	Pathology/lab	80047–89398, P2028–P9615, ATP02-ATP22
	Physical medicine	97001–98943
	Radiology	70010–79999, R0070–R0076
	Other ancillary	36415–36416; 99000-99002
Other professional services	Includes services and items, such as oxygen therapy, durable medical equipment, and prosthetic devices.	B4034–B9999, C1300–C9899, G0027– G9142, M0064–M0301, Q0035–Q9968, S0012–S9999, T1000–T5999, V5008–V5299, V5336–V5364, W0000–ZZZZZ; 99026-99091

Source: GAO analysis of the 2010 Healthcare Common Procedural Coding System and Health Care Cost and Utilization Report: 2010. Health Care Cost Institute (2012). | GAO-15-481

We excluded dental and behavioral health services from our analysis because these services may be contracted out by managed care organizations (MCO) and provided on a fee-for-service (FFS) basis. Additionally, Mathematica reported concerns regarding the quality of managed care behavioral health data.[34]

Step 3: Utilization Calculation

For each service provided to each beneficiary described in steps 1 and 2 above, we calculated the number of services per beneficiary per year. This is defined as the number of services that beneficiaries enrolled in comprehensive managed care plans used in a year (includes users and nonusers enrolled in comprehensive managed care plans within the state).[35]

The number of services per beneficiary, per year is calculated as follows:

$$\left[\frac{\textit{Total number of managed care professional services}}{\textit{Number of managed care beneficiary months of enrollment in the states, 2010}}\right] \times 12$$

We presented service utilization patterns for adults and children by state, by service category, and by the length of beneficiary enrollment—in particular, whether beneficiaries were enrolled in a comprehensive managed care plan for a full or partial year. We then further grouped partial-year beneficiaries into monthly increments—1-3, 4-6, and 7-11 months—to determine whether there were differences in utilization patterns by the varying lengths of enrollment.

Services per beneficiary, per year is the product of two additional measures:

1. User Rate: the percent of beneficiaries who used at least one service in a year, is calculated as follows:

$$\left[\frac{\textit{Total number of months for beneficiaries with at least one service}}{\textit{Total months of managed care beneficiary enrollment in the state, 2010}}\right] \times 12$$

2. Services per user, per year: the number of services used, calculated among service users. The number of services per user, per year is calculated as follows:

$$\left[\frac{\textit{Total number of managed care professional service}}{\textit{Number of user months of managed care enrollment in the state, 2010}}\right] \times 12$$

In addition to services used by beneficiaries enrolled in a comprehensive managed care plan, we also calculated the extent to which the beneficiaries in our analysis received professional services paid on a FFS basis while they were enrolled in a comprehensive managed care plan.

See http://www.gao.gov/products/GAO-15-481 for further detail on these measures and the FFS data.

Study Limitations and State Technical Comments

The results we present are based on data reported to CMS by the 19 states in our analysis. We did not independently verify whether the individual MCOs in these states submitted complete and accurate data on the enrollment and services for beneficiaries enrolled in comprehensive managed care.

To better understand the factors that may affect service utilization, we asked representatives from each state to comment on the accuracy and completeness of the state's 2010 managed care data submitted to CMS.[36] Thirteen of the 19 selected states responded to our request.[37] These states met our criteria for inclusion, as well as the minimum threshold for the number of services per adult or child beneficiary used by Mathematica to assess the completeness of each state's data.[38] Nevertheless, of these 13 states, 4 states indicated that they may have submitted incomplete enrollment or encounter data in 2010, citing a variety of reasons.[39] For example, 1 state indicated its Medicaid managed care program was in the process of major changes and service data were likely not complete. Another state indicated that, in calendar year 2010, some of the state's managed care data were not reported due to quality problems. Officials from the remaining 9 states noted their results either seemed reasonable based on their knowledge of their state's Medicaid managed care program or that the managed care data they submitted to CMS for 2010 was believed to be accurate.

The results we present for the 19 states in our analysis are not representative of all states and their managed care programs, nor do our results draw any conclusions regarding whether the level of service utilization identified is appropriate. There are a number of state-specific factors—such as differences in beneficiary health status and provider supply—that could contribute to variation in service utilization across the states. For example, officials from 1 state noted that the state's MCOs were limited to certain geographical areas of the state. As such, geographic variation in provider access, which can be driven by the breadth of an MCO's network and the availability of providers in a given geographic area, can affect the type and amount of services used by beneficiaries in Medicaid managed care.

APPENDIX II: SERVICE UTILIZATION PATTERNS FOR BENEFICIARIES IN COMPREHENSIVE MANAGED CARE, 2010

The tables below provide the number of services per beneficiary per year for adults and children by state, service category, and length of enrollment.

Based on our analysis of encounter data, the number of professional services utilized per beneficiary per year reported by the 19 selected states for adults enrolled in comprehensive managed care plans in 2010 ranged from about 13 to 55; the range for children was generally lower, from about 6 to 16. States varied in how adult and child utilization of professional services were distributed across service categories. In addition, service utilization for both adults and children varied by whether beneficiaries were enrolled in comprehensive managed care plans for all of 2010 or part of the year.[40] In particular, for nearly all states in our analysis, partial-year child beneficiaries utilized significantly more services overall than those enrolled for the full year.

Table 3. Adult Professional Service Utilization in Selected States, 2010

		Service categories (percent of total managed care services)			
State	**Total managed care services**	**Evaluation and management**	**Procedural**	**Ancillary**	**Other professional**
RI	13	5 (38)	2 (18)	5 (37)	0.9 (7)
IL	14	4 (26)	1 (8)	9 (65)	0.1 (1)
FL	14	4 (25)	2 (11)	9 (62)	0.3 (2)
CT	15	3 (19)	3 (17)	8 (55)	1.3 (9)
NY	18	4 (23)	3 (16)	11 (59)	0.3 (2)
OR	18	6 (32)	3 (17)	9 (49)	0.4 (2)

State	Total managed care services	Evaluation and management	Procedural	Ancillary	Other professional
NM	20	6 (30)	3 (18)	10 (49)	0.7 (4)
IN	20	4 (23)	4 (23)	10 (52)	0.5 (2)
NE	20	6 (31)	4 (21)	9 (47)	0.3 (1)
TN	23	7 (30)	4 (15)	12 (52)	0.7 (3)
AZ	24	7 (29)	3 (13)	10 (43)	3.7 (15)
VA	24	7 (29)	3 (14)	13 (54)	0.6 (2)
MI	25	7 (26)	4 (15)	14 (54)	1.2 (5)
DE	26	8 (32)	4 (14)	12 (45)	2.4 (9)
WA	26	6 (21)	3 (12)	17 (65)	0.3 (1)
GA	27	7 (27)	4 (15)	15 (55)	0.5 (2)
MN	27	6 (22)	5 (20)	14 (52)	1.8 (7)
KY	32	10 (31)	3 (11)	18 (57)	0.3 (1)
TX	55	15 (27)	6 (10)	34 (62)	0.8 (2)
Median	23	6	3	11	0.6

Source: GAO analysis of Medicaid Analytic eXtract data for calendar year 2010. | GAO-15-481

Notes: Beneficiaries included in our analysis were eligible to receive full Medicaid benefits and were enrolled in a comprehensive managed care plan in at least one month during calendar year 2010. We excluded beneficiaries who were enrolled in a comprehensive managed care plan if during the calendar year of our analysis they had other sources of health coverage in addition to Medicaid. We focused our analysis on professional services and excluded dental and behavioral health services and any services paid on a fee-for-service basis. Evaluation and management services include services such as office visits and emergency room and critical care services. Procedural services include services such as surgery and ophthalmology. Ancillary services include services such as pathology and lab services, and anesthesiology. Other professional services include services such as oxygen therapy, hospital-mandated on-call service, and other services that are not otherwise classified in the categories above. See appendix I for more information. For the percentage of partial- year beneficiaries by state, see appendix III. Numbers are rounded to the nearest whole number except for the other professional services category. The percentages of total services in each state attributable to specific service categories were calculated based on unrounded data. A detailed, interactive display of the data used to support our findings is available at http://www.gao.gov/products/GAO-15-481.

Table 4. Adult Professional Service Utilization in Selected States, Partial-Year Beneficiaries Compared with Full-Year Beneficiaries, 2010

State	Full-year beneficiaries					Partial-year beneficiaries (percent difference)				
	Total managed care services	Evaluation and management	Procedural	Ancillary	Other professional	Total managed care services	Evaluation and management	Procedural	Ancillary	Other professional
DE	28.5	8.9	3.9	12.8	3.7	24.1 (-15)	7.7 (-14)	3.4 (-14)	11.1 (-13)	1.9 (-33)
AZ	25.0	7.1	3.3	10.8	1.3	21.5 (-14)	6.4 (-10)	2.7 (-17)	8.9 (-18)	3.5 (-7)
RI	13.8	5.3	2.4	5.0	2.9	12.2 (-12)	4.6 (-13)	2.3 (-6)	4.6 (-8)	0.7 (-34)
TN	24.1	7.2	3.8	12.3	0.4	21.5 (-11)	6.1 (-16)	3.2 (-14)	11.6 (-5)	0.6 (-28)
NY	18.7	4.3	3.0	11.1	0.4	16.9 (-10)	4.1 (-5)	2.8 (-7)	9.7 (-12)	0.3 (-6)
FL	15.1	3.8	1.6	9.3	0.1	14.0 (-8)	3.5 (-8)	1.5 (-5)	8.6 (-7)	0.3 (-23)
OR	18.8	6.4	3.1	8.9	0.5	18.2 (-3)	5.3 (-17)	3.2 (4)	9.3 (5)	0.4 (-16)
CT	14.7	2.8	2.5	8.1	0.4	14.2 (-3)	2.6 (-9)	2.5 (2)	7.8 (-3)	1.2 (-2)
MN	27.1	5.8	5.2	14.0	1.2	27.7 (2)	6.1 (5)	5.5 (7)	14.4 (3)	1.7 (-19)
NM	19.4	6.1	3.4	9.3	2.1	19.9 (3)	5.3 (-13)	3.7 (9)	10.2 (10)	0.7 (2)
WA	25.9	6.2	2.9	16.4	0.2	26.7 (3)	5.3 (-14)	3.2 (10)	17.7 (8)	0.3 (-8)
MI	24.4	6.6	3.5	13.1	0.7	25.9 (6)	6.5 (-2)	4.0 (15)	14.1 (7)	1.3 (8)
VA	22.6	6.9	3.0	12.1	0.3	25.2 (12)	7.1 (3)	3.8 (25)	13.8 (14)	0.5 (-14)
IL	12.6	3.5	1.1	7.9	0.5	14.9 (18)	3.6 (4)	1.2 (8)	10.0 (27)	0.1 (-5)
NE	17.3	6.0	3.5	7.6	1.1	20.8 (20)	6.2 (3)	4.3 (23)	10.1 (32)	0.3 (20)

State	Full-year beneficiaries					Partial-year beneficiaries (percent difference)				
	Total managed care services	Evaluation and management	Procedural	Ancillary	Other professional	Total managed care services	Evaluation and management	Procedural	Ancillary	Other professional
GA	23.4	7.6	3.6	11.8	0.8	28.1 (20)	7.1 (-7)	4.3 (19)	16.2 (37)	0.5 (34)
KY	28.1	8.9	3.2	15.6	0.8	34.9 (24)	10.8 (20)	3.5 (9)	20.3 (31)	0.3 (-26)
IN	16.5	4.3	3.3	8.4	0.6	22.9 (39)	4.7 (11)	5.5 (66)	12.2 (45)	0.5 (-7)
TX	31.7	9.1	3.8	18.0	0.4	56.4 (78)	14.9 (64)	5.8 (53)	34.8 (94)	0.8 (-2)

Source: GAO analysis of Medicaid Analytic eXtract data for calendar year 2010. | GAO-15-481

Notes: Beneficiaries included in our analysis were eligible to receive full Medicaid benefits and were enrolled in a comprehensive managed care plan in at least one month during calendar year 2010. Partial-year beneficiaries are defined as those enrolled in a comprehensive managed care plan in calendar year 2010 for a period of less than 12 months. We weighted our results by the number of months each beneficiary was enrolled in comprehensive managed care in calendar year 2010 to account for beneficiaries who may have been enrolled for only part of the year. We excluded beneficiaries who were enrolled in a comprehensive managed care plan if during the calendar year of our analysis they had other sources of health coverage in addition to Medicaid. We focused our analysis on professional services and excluded dental and behavioral health services and any services paid on a fee-for-service basis. Evaluation and management services include services such as office visits and emergency room and critical care services. Procedural services include services such as surgery and ophthalmology. Ancillary services include services such as pathology and lab services, and anesthesiology. Other professional services include services such as oxygen therapy, hospital-mandated on-call service, and other services that are not otherwise classified in the categories above. See appendix I for more information. For the percentage of partial-year beneficiaries by state, see appendix III. Numbers are rounded to the nearest tenth except for the other professional services category. The percent difference for each state was calculated based on unrounded data. A detailed, interactive display of the data used to support our findings is available at http://www.gao.gov/products/GAO-15-481.

Table 5. Child Professional Service Utilization in Selected States, 2010

		Service categories (percent of total managed care services)			
State	Total managed care services	Evaluation and management	Procedural	Ancillary	Other professional
IL	6	2 (35)	2 (29)	2 (36)	0.0 (1)
RI	8	4 (45)	3 (32)	1 (18)	0.4 (5)
FL	8	3 (38)	2 (30)	2 (29)	0.3 (4)
NE	9	4 (42)	3 (34)	2 (22)	0.2 (2)
CT	9	3 (33)	2 (28)	3 (29)	1.0 (11)
WA	9	3 (37)	3 (29)	3 (32)	0.2 (2)
OR	10	4 (39)	4 (41)	2 (17)	0.3 (3)
VA	10	4 (39)	3 (33)	3 (25)	0.2 (2)
NY	11	4 (34)	4 (32)	4 (32)	0.1 (1)
IN	11	5 (43)	3 (30)	3 (25)	0.2 (2)
NM	11	4 (37)	4 (37)	2 (18)	0.9 (8)
AZ	12	4 (33)	3 (25)	2 (20)	2.5 (21)
GA	12	5 (45)	4 (34)	2 (20)	0.2 (1)
DE	12	5 (39)	5 (39)	2 (18)	0.5 (4)
MI	13	4 (34)	4 (34)	3 (27)	0.6 (5)
TN	13	4 (35)	4 (35)	3 (26)	0.5 (4)
KY	13	5 (38)	4 (33)	4 (27)	0.2 (2)
TX	15	6 (37)	6 (41)	3 (19)	0.5 (3)
MN	16	5 (29)	6 (36)	4 (23)	1.8 (12)
Median	11	4	4	3	0.3

Source: GAO analysis of Medicaid Analytic eXtract data for calendar year 2010. | GAO-15-481

Notes: Beneficiaries included in our analysis were eligible to receive full Medicaid benefits and were enrolled in a comprehensive managed care plan in at least one month during calendar year 2010. We excluded beneficiaries who were enrolled in a comprehensive managed care plan if during the calendar year of our analysis they had other sources of health coverage in addition to Medicaid. We focused our analysis on professional services and excluded dental and behavioral health services and any services paid on a fee-for-service basis. Evaluation and management services include services such as office visits and emergency room and critical care services. Procedural services include services such as surgery and ophthalmology. Ancillary services include services such as pathology and lab services, and anesthesiology. Other professional services include services such as oxygen therapy, hospital-mandated on-call service, and other services that are not otherwise classified in the categories above. See appendix I for more information. For the percentage of partial-year beneficiaries by state, see appendix III. Numbers are rounded to the nearest whole number except for the other professional services category. The percentages of total services in each state attributable to specific service categories were calculated based on unrounded data. A detailed, interactive display of the data used to support our findings is available at http://www.gao.gov/products/GAO-15-481.

Table 6. Child Professional Service Utilization in Selected States, Partial-Year Beneficiaries Compared with Full-Year Beneficiaries, 2010

State	Full-year beneficiaries					Partial-year beneficiaries (percent difference)				
	Total managed care services	Evaluation and management	Procedural	Ancillary	Other professional	Total managed care services	Evaluation and management	Procedural	Ancillary	Other professional
AZ	11.8	3.9	2.9	2.4	2.7	11.3 (-5)	3.9 (1)	3.2 (11)	2.2 (-7)	1.94 (-27)
TX	15.1	5.5	6.0	3.0	0.6	15.7 (4)	5.9 (7)	6.5 (9)	2.8 (-7)	0.44 (-30)
RI	7.9	3.5	2.5	1.5	0.4	8.2 (4)	3.7 (7)	2.7 (7)	1.4 (-6)	0.39 (-3)
TN	12.6	4.4	4.4	3.4	0.5	13.2 (5)	5.0 (16)	4.7 (7)	3.2 (-7)	0.32 (-37)
NY	10.8	3.6	3.4	3.7	0.1	11.5 (6)	4.2 (15)	4.0 (19)	3.1 (-15)	0.14 (3)
MN	15.0	4.2	5.4	3.5	1.9	16.0 (7)	4.7 (14)	5.9 (8)	3.5 (1)	1.82 (-3)
DE	11.8	4.5	4.5	2.2	0.5	12.6 (7)	5.1 (12)	4.9 (8)	2.1 (-5)	0.49 (-2)
KY	12.5	4.6	4.1	3.6	0.2	13.6 (9)	5.5 (20)	4.5 (11)	3.4 (-6)	0.18 (-15)
MI	12.0	4.1	4.0	3.4	0.6	13.5 (12)	4.7 (16)	4.7 (17)	3.5 (4)	0.61 (1)
FL	7.6	2.9	2.1	2.2	0.3	8.7 (15)	3.2 (11)	2.7 (28)	2.5 (11)	0.27 (-18)
IN	10.5	4.3	3.2	2.7	0.2	12.0 (15)	5.3 (23)	3.6 (13)	2.9 (5)	0.22 (2)
CT	8.5	2.7	2.3	2.6	0.9	9.8 (15)	3.6 (35)	2.7 (17)	2.3 (-12)	1.16 (26)
OR	9.1	3.5	3.7	1.6	0.3	10.5 (16)	4.2 (22)	4.4 (20)	1.6 (0)	0.27 (-19)
WA	8.7	3.3	2.5	2.8	0.2	10.5 (20)	3.8 (15)	3.2 (29)	3.4 (20)	0.18 (4)
GA	10.7	4.7	3.5	2.3	0.1	13.1 (22)	6.0 (26)	4.6 (30)	2.4 (5)	0.15 (1)
VA	9.5	3.8	3.0	2.6	0.2	11.8 (24)	4.7 (24)	4.3 (44)	2.6 (2)	0.23 (-5)
NM	10.7	3.9	3.8	2.1	0.9	14.1 (32)	5.3 (35)	5.6 (50)	2.1 (1)	1.03 (15)
NE	7.3	3.1	2.4	1.6	0.2	9.6 (33)	4.0 (30)	3.4 (38)	2.1 (32)	0.21 (22)
IL	5.3	1.9	1.5	1.9	0.0	7.7 (44)	2.6 (35)	2.2 (44)	2.9 (55)	0.05 (29)

Source: GAO analysis of Medicaid Analytic eXtract data for calendar year 2010. | GAO-15-481

Notes: Beneficiaries included in our analysis were eligible to receive full Medicaid benefits and were enrolled in a comprehensive managed care plan in at least one month during calendar year 2010. Partial-year beneficiaries are defined as those enrolled in a comprehensive managed care plan in calendar year 2010 for a period of less than 12 months. We weighted our results by the number of months each beneficiary was enrolled in comprehensive managed care in calendar year 2010 to account for beneficiaries who may have been enrolled for only part of the year. We excluded beneficiaries who were enrolled in a comprehensive managed care plan if during the calendar year of our analysis they had other sources of health coverage in addition to Medicaid. We focused our analysis on professional services and excluded dental and behavioral health services and any services paid on a fee-for-service basis. Evaluation and management services include services such as office visits and emergency room and critical care services. Procedural services include services such as surgery and ophthalmology. Ancillary services include services such as pathology and lab services, and anesthesiology. Other professional services include services such as oxygen therapy, hospital-mandated on-call service, and other services that are not otherwise classified in the categories above. See appendix I for more information. For the percentage of partial-year beneficiaries by state, see appendix III. Numbers are rounded to the nearest tenth except for the other professional services category. The percent difference for each state was calculated based on unrounded data. A detailed, interactive display of the data used to support our findings is available at http://www.gao.gov/products/GAO-15-481.

APPENDIX III: PERCENTAGE OF PARTIAL-YEAR BENEFICIARIES IN SELECTED STATES IN 2010

State	Adults	Children
Arizona	45%	37%
Connecticut	42	35
Delaware	66	58
Florida	79	61
Georgia	82	62
Illinois	61	52
Indiana	68	50
Kentucky	76	49
Michigan	67	51
Minnesota	76	71
Nebraska	88	77
New Mexico	46	35
New York	51	43
Oregon	71	56
Rhode Island	55	47
Tennessee	48	32
Texas	97	72
Virginia	73	52
Washington	79	45

Source: GAO analysis of Medicaid Analytic eXtract data for calendar year 2010. | GAO-15-481

Notes: Beneficiaries included in our analysis were eligible to receive full Medicaid benefits and were enrolled in a comprehensive managed care plan in at least one month during calendar year 2010. We excluded beneficiaries who were enrolled in a comprehensive managed care plan if during the calendar year of our analysis they had other sources of health coverage in addition to Medicaid.

End Notes

[1] The MCO, in turn, pays the provider for the services they provided.

[2] Medicaid serves low-income and medically needy individuals. Under PPACA, states were allowed to expand eligibility for Medicaid under their state plan to most nonelderly, nonpregnant adults who are not eligible for Medicare and whose income is at or below 133 percent of the federal poverty level. PPACA also provides for a 5 percent disregard when calculating income for determining Medicaid eligibility for this population, which effectively increases this income level to 138 percent of the federal poverty level. Pub. L.

No. 111-148, § 2001(a)(1), 124 Stat. 119, 271 (2010). For purposes of this report, references to PPACA include the amendments made by the Health Care and Education Reconciliation Act of 2010, Pub. L. No. 111-152, 124 Stat. 1029 (2010).

[3] Mathematica Policy Research first reported in 2012 that 2007-2010 Medicaid encounter data, as reported in MAX, were suitable for research purposes. PPACA strengthened the requirement that Medicaid MCOs provide encounter data to states by withholding federal matching payments from states that do not report encounter data to CMS in a timely manner. Pub. L. No. 111-148, §§ 6402(c), 6504(b), 124 Stat. 119, 757, 777 (2010) (codified at 42 U.S.C. §§ 1396b(i)(25), (m)(2)(A)(xi)).

[4] The MAX data files for each state contain information on Medicaid eligibility, service utilization, and payment for each Medicaid beneficiary during a given calendar year. These files are derived from each state's Medicaid Statistical Information System (MSIS) data files and have been processed by CMS's contractor into a research friendly format. We obtained MAX data from CMS in November 2013.

[5] In the 19 selected states, we did not independently verify whether individual MCOs in these states submitted complete and accurate enrollment and encounter data.

[6] We excluded these 31 states and the District of Columbia for the following reasons: (1) no adults or children were enrolled in comprehensive managed care plans, according to MAX (13 states); (2) MAX data were unavailable at the time we began our analysis (11 states); (3) we determined that the data were unreliable such as if fewer than 30 percent of beneficiaries used at least one service (6 states); and (4) services were not reported using a standard coding convention, namely the Health Care Common Procedural Coding System (HCPCS) (2 states). See appendix I for more detail on which states we excluded and why.

[7] Within the four broad categories of professional services, E/M services include preventive services, office and inpatient visits, consultations, and emergency room or critical care visits; procedural services include allergy, cardiovascular, ophthalmology, surgery-administered drugs (including chemotherapy), and immunizations/injections; ancillary services include pathology and lab services, physical medicine, radiology, and anesthesia services; and other professional services include oxygen therapy, hospital-mandated on- call service, and other services that are not otherwise classified in the categories above. We, in large part, utilized the Health Care Cost Institute's methodology for grouping professional services based on a range of HCPCS codes. These codes are used by providers to bill for professional services.

[8] While our beneficiary population was comprised of individuals enrolled in comprehensive managed care plans, our utilization analysis included all state-reported encounters for the services we reviewed, regardless of whether they were provided through a comprehensive managed care plan or other types of managed care.

[9] We did not compare our results to, for example, utilization in Medicaid fee for service (FFS) or commercial insurance because differences in population characteristics made it difficult to find a suitable comparison group.

[10] See GAO, *Medicaid: Assessment of Variation among States in Per-Enrollee Spending*, GAO-14-456 (Washington, D.C.: June 16, 2014).

[11] See GAO, *Medicare: Private Sector Initiatives to Bundle Hospital and Physician Payments for an Episode of Care*, GAO-11-126R (Washington, D.C.: Jan. 31, 2011).

[12] The Balanced Budget Act of 1997 required states to submit detailed individual enrollee encounter data to CMS as a condition of receiving federal reimbursement for mechanized claims processing systems. Pub. L. No. 105-33, § 4753, 111 Stat. 251, 525 (1997) (codified at 42 U.S.C. § 1396b(r)(1)(F)).

[13] Studies using data prior to 2009 have raised questions regarding the accuracy and completeness of encounter data or avoided using encounter data. See The Lewin Group, General Dynamics, *Evaluating Emergency Department Utilization: For Researchers using the Centers for Medicare & Medicaid Services Chronic Condition Data Warehouse* (Falls Church, VA.: May 2012); and *Medicaid Enrollees' Utilization of Ambulatory Care Services*

For Researchers using the Centers for Medicare & Medicaid Services' Chronic Condition Data Warehouse (Falls Church, VA.: Sept. 2012).

[14] See GAO, *Medicare Advantage: CMS Should Fully Develop Plans for Encounter Data and Assess Data Quality before Use*, GAO-14-571 (Washington, D.C.: July 31, 2014).

[15] Pub. L. No. 111-148, §§ 6402(c), 6504(b), 124 Stat. 119, 757, 777 (2010) (codified at 42 U.S.C. §§ 1396b(i)(25), (m)(2)(A)(xi)).

[16] See GAO-14-456 and *Medicaid Payment: Comparisons of Selected Services under Fee-for-Service, Managed Care, and Private Insurance*, GAO-14-533 (Washington, D.C.: Jul 15, 2014).

[17] State Medicaid programs are required to cover certain "mandatory benefits," and can choose to provide other "optional benefits."

[18] See GAO-14-533.

[19] Variation in access to providers can also occur for beneficiaries who receive services on a FFS basis.

[20] See http://www.gao.gov/products/GAO-15-481 for the percentage of adult beneficiaries in each state who used at least one professional service and for the number of services they used.

[21] See http://www.gao.gov/products/GAO-15-481 for further detail on the number and percentage of professional services adult beneficiaries in comprehensive managed care received on a FFS basis by state.

[22] The percentage of partial-year adult beneficiaries varied considerably across selected states. See appendix III for more detail.

[23] See http://www.gao.gov/products/GAO-15-481 for the percentage of child beneficiaries in each state who used at least one professional service and the number of services used among beneficiaries who used services.

[24] See http://www.gao.gov/products/GAO-15-481 for further detail on the number and percentage of professional services child beneficiaries in comprehensive managed care received on a FFS basis by state.

[25] The percentage of partial-year child beneficiaries varied considerably across selected states. See appendix III for more detail.

[26] We obtained MAX data from the Centers for Medicare & Medicaid Services (CMS) in November 2013.

[27] The MAX data files for each state contain information on Medicaid eligibility, service utilization, and payment for each Medicaid beneficiary during a given calendar year. These files are derived from each state's Medicaid Statistical Information System (MSIS) data files and have been processed by CMS's contractor into a research friendly format. MAX includes five files: a Person Summary—PS—file, which contains one record for every individual enrolled for at least one day during the year as well as demographic data (e.g. date of birth, gender, race), basis of eligibility, and monthly enrollment status; and four claims files. The four claims files—Inpatient, Institutional Long-Term Care, Prescription Drug, and Other Services—OT—include claims and managed care service (also known as encounters) data for Medicaid beneficiaries in a given calendar year within a state.

[28] See Mathematica Policy Research, *Medicaid Policy Brief: Assessing the Usability of MAX 2008 Encounter Data for Enrollees in Comprehensive Managed Care 2008*, Brief 7 (Washington, D.C.: July 2012); *Medicaid Policy Brief: Assessing the Usability of Encounter Data for Enrollees in Comprehensive Managed Care Across MAX 2007–2009*, Brief 15 (Washington, D.C.: December 2012); *Medicaid Analytic eXtract 2008 Encounter Data Chartbook* (Washington, D.C.: 2013); *The Medicaid Analytic eXtract 2010 Chartbook (Washington, D.C.:* 2014); and *Medicaid Policy Brief: The Availability and Usability of Behavioral Health Organization Encounter Data in MAX 2009*, Brief 14 (Washington, D.C.: July 2013).

[29] We also solicited input from representatives of these states on the accuracy of the MAX data we analyzed. See state technical comments later described in this appendix. In addition, for

these states, we excluded duplicate records in the MAX data files that could lead to an overcounting of services.

[30] The majority of states report services using HCPCS.

[31] We used the MAX Basis of Eligibility variable to determine whether beneficiaries were full benefit adults or children.

[32] For example, we excluded individuals that do not receive full Medicaid coverage, such as undocumented individuals who are eligible for emergency services only, individuals who receive only family planning services, and those who receive only premium assistance for the purchase of private insurance.

[33] See Health Care Cost Institute, *Health Care Cost and Utilization Report: 2010* (Washington, D.C.: May 2012).

[34] A Mathematica study indicated that encounter data on behavioral health services are often incomplete and unreliable. See Mathematica Policy Research, *Medicaid Policy Brief: The Availability and Usability of Behavioral Health Organization Encounter Data in MAX 2009*, Brief 14 (Washington, D.C.: July 2013).

[35] When calculating utilization, we weighted our results by the number of months each beneficiary was enrolled in comprehensive managed care in calendar year 2010 to account for beneficiaries who may have been enrolled for only part of the year. While our beneficiary population was comprised of individuals enrolled in comprehensive managed care plans, our utilization analysis included all state-reported encounters for the services we reviewed, regardless of whether they were provided through a comprehensive managed care plan or other types of managed care.

[36] States submit data to CMS through MSIS. Each state's MSIS data files have been processed by CMS's contractor into MAX's more research-friendly format.

[37] The states that did not respond to our request are Connecticut, Georgia, Minnesota, New Mexico, Oregon, and Rhode Island.

[38] All 19 states included in our analysis also met Mathematica's quality measure of having a complete procedure code. Mathematica's four remaining quality measures did not directly affect our analysis.

[39] The states that indicated they may have submitted incomplete data are Delaware, Florida, Illinois, and Nebraska.

[40] See appendix III for the percentage of partial-year adult and child beneficiaries by state.

INDEX

A

B

C

D

E

F

G

H

I

L

M

N

O

P

Q

R

S